EPPING

DK BACKPACK BOOKS

1,001 FACTS ABOUT
PLANET EARTH

NUCLEAR
FISSION

ISLAND ARC

COMPOSITE VOLCANO

SHIELD
VOLCANO

BACKPACK BOOKS

1,001 FACTS ABOUT

PLANET EARTH

Written by CALLY HALL and SCARLETT O'HARA
With additional material by JEN GREEN

SATELLITE
PICTURE
OF EARTH'S
OZONE HOLE

ONION-LAYERING

CARBONIFEROUS FOREST

A Dorling Kindersley Book

LONDON, NEW YORK, MUNICH,
MELBOURNE, DELHI

Project editor Clare Lister
Senior designer Adrienne Hutchinson
Assistant designer Joanne Little
Assistant editor Sarah Goulding
Senior editorial co-ordinator Camilla Hallinan
Senior design co-ordinator Sophia M Tampakopoulos Turner
DTP Jill Bunyan
Category publisher Sue Grabham
Production Linda Dare
With thanks to the original team:
Art editor Susan Downing
Senior editor Laura Buller
Picture research Charlotte Bush, Christine Rista

First published in Great Britain in 2003
by Dorling Kindersley Limited
80 Strand, London WC2R 0RL
A Penguin Company

A CIP catalogue record for this book is available from the British Library

ISBN 0 7513 4421 4

Colour reproduction by Colourscan
Printed and bound in Singapore by Star Standard

See our complete catalogue at
www.dk.com

CONTENTS

PLANET EARTH

HOW THE EARTH WAS FORMED

ABOUT 5,000 MILLION years ago our Solar System began to take shape. The Sun and the nine planets formed from a cloud of dust and gas swirling in space. Some scientists believe that the centre of this cloud cooled and contracted to form the Sun. Gravity pulled the planets from the rest of the cloud. Other scientists suggest that the dust cloud formed asteroids that joined together to make the Sun and planets.

1 FORMING THE SUN
A spinning cloud of gas and dust contracted to form the Sun. Cooler matter from this dust cloud combined to shape the planets.

A dense atmosphere of cosmic gases surrounded the Earth.

2 FORMING THE EARTH
The Earth's radio-activity caused the surface to melt. Lighter minerals floated to the surface and heavier elements, such as iron and nickel, sank to form the Earth's core.

3 THE EARTH'S CRUST
About 4,000 million years ago, the Earth's crust began to form. Blocks of cooling, solid rock floated on a molten rock layer. The rock sometimes sank and remelted before rising again.

EARTH FACTS

• The Earth orbits the Sun at 29.8 km/sec (18.5 miles/sec).

• Oceans cover 70.8% of the Earth's surface.

• Earth is not a sphere – it bulges in the middle.

• The Earth completes a turn on its axis every 23 hours, 56 minutes.

COMPOSITION OF THE EARTH

The elements here are divided by weight. Earth's crust consists mostly of oxygen, silicon, and aluminium. Heavier metals such as iron and nickel are found in the core.

Other elements less than 1%
Aluminium 1.1%
Sulphur 1.9%
Nickel 2.4%
Magnesium 13%
Silicon 15%
Oxygen 30%
Iron 35%

4 MAKING THE ATMOSPHERE
The Earth's crust thickened. It took several million years for volcanic gases to form the atmosphere. Water vapour condensed to make oceans.

6 THE EARTH TODAY
Earth's unique conditions are just right to support a variety of life. Our planet, though, continues to change. Tectonic plates are moving, pulling some continents nearer and pushing others farther apart.

5 LAND FORMS
About 3,500 million years ago proto-continents formed on the crust. Today's continents look very different.

THE EARTH IN SPACE

EARTH IS A DENSE rocky planet, third nearest to the
Sun, and tiny compared with Jupiter and Saturn.
While Earth rotates on its axis each day, it also
orbits the Sun each year, held in orbit by the
Sun's gravity. One moon revolves around the
Earth. From space the Earth looks blue and
calm but under its oceans, deep beneath the
crust, the Earth's core is fiery and white-hot.

MERCURY
- 87.96 days to orbit Sun
- diameter 4,878 km
  (3,032 miles)

EARTH
- 365.26 days to orbit Sun
- diameter 12,756 km
  (7,928 miles)
- 1 moon

THE SOLAR SYSTEM
Our Solar System consists of nine
planets, as well as moons, asteroids,
comets, meteorites, dust, and gas. All
of these orbit a central star – the Sun.

JUPITER

MERCURY EARTH
VENUS MARS

MARS
- 686.98 days to orbit Sun
- diameter 6,786 km
  (4,217 miles)
- 2 moons

The Great
Red Spot is a
cyclone.

VENUS
- 224.7 days to orbit Sun
- diameter 12,102 km
  (7,521 miles)

SUN
- diameter 1,391,980 km (865,121 miles)

JUPITER
- 11.86 years to orbit Sun
- diameter 142,984 km
  (88,865 miles)
- 16 moons
- 1 ring

The Earth tilts at an angle of 23.5°.

This side of the planet has its winter.

EARTH'S ORBIT

As the Earth spins on its axis, it also orbits the Sun. When the northern hemisphere faces the Sun it has its summer. At the same time the southern hemisphere faces away from the Sun and has its winter. The equator faces towards the Sun most of the time and there are no significant seasonal changes there.

DISTANCE FROM THE SUN		
PLANET	MILLION KM	MILLION MILES
Mercury	58	36
Venus	108	67
Earth	150	93
Mars	228	142
Jupiter	778	484
Saturn	1,427	887
Uranus	2,871	1,784
Neptune	4,497	2,795
Pluto	5,914	3,675

Saturn's rings are made of pieces of icy rock and dust.

SATURN

Uranus rotates on its side.

PLUTO
- 248.54 years to orbit Sun
- diameter 2,300 km (1,429 miles)
- 1 moon

NEPTUNE

PLUTO

URANUS

The Great Dark Spot is a huge storm.

Little is known about Pluto – it is probably icy.

SATURN
- 29.46 years to orbit Sun
- diameter 120,536 km (74,914 miles)
- 18 moons
- 7 rings

URANUS
- 84 years to orbit Sun
- diameter 51,118 km (31,770 miles)
- 15 moons
- 11 rings

NEPTUNE
- 164.79 years to orbit Sun
- diameter 49,528 km (30,782 miles)
- 8 moons
- 4 rings

EARTH'S MAGNETIC FIELD

THE EARTH BEHAVES like a giant magnet. Molten iron
and nickel flow in the Earth's outer core and produce
an electric current. This electricity creates a
magnetic field, or magnetosphere, that extends into
space. Like a magnet, the Earth has two magnetic
poles. From time to time, the magnetic poles reverse
polarity. The last time they changed was about
700,000 years ago. No one knows why
this happens.

MAGNETIC POLES
North and south geographical
poles lie at either end of the
Earth's axis (the invisible line
around which the Earth turns).
The magnetic poles' position
varies over time. It is the Earth's
magnetic field that causes a
compass needle to point north.

MAGNETIC FACTS
• Whales and birds
use the Earth's
magnetic field to help
them navigate.

• Every second the Sun
sheds at least a million
tonnes (tons) of matter
into the solar wind.

Geographic pole

Magnetic pole

Earth

Axis

*Invisible lines of magnetic
force form a pattern around
the Earth. Closer lines reveal
a stronger magnetic field*

*North and south
magnetic poles are
always near to
north and south
geographical poles*

MAGNETOSPHERE

Earth's magnetosphere extends about 60,000 km (37,000 miles) into space. It protects the Earth from some of the Sun's most harmful particles.

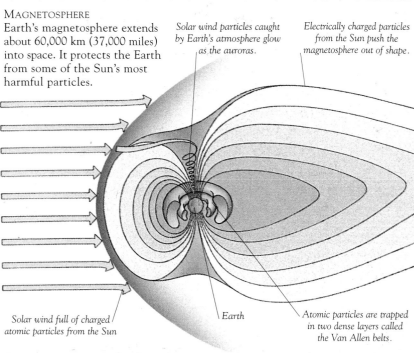

Solar wind particles caught by Earth's atmosphere glow as the auroras.

Electrically charged particles from the Sun push the magnetosphere out of shape.

Solar wind full of charged atomic particles from the Sun

Earth

Atomic particles are trapped in two dense layers called the Van Allen belts.

The polarity of new crust reverses between north and south.

MAGNETIC CRUST

New oceanic crust rises out of the Earth at mid-oceanic ridges. As the rock solidifies, a record of the Earth's magnetism is locked into it. Earth's changing polarities lead to a magnetic pattern in the rock, symmetrical either side of the spreading ridge.

15

EARTH'S ATMOSPHERE

THE EARTH IS WRAPPED in a blanket of gases called the atmosphere. This thin layer protects the Earth from the Sun's fierce rays and from the hostile conditions of outer space. There are five layers in the Earth's atmosphere before the air merges with outer space. The layers hold air and water vapour that support life, and our weather and climate.

A THIN LAYER
The Earth's atmosphere is actually a thin band around the Earth. If the Earth were an orange, the atmosphere would be as thin as the skin of the orange.

EXOSPHERE
• begins at 900 km (560 miles)
• thin layer before spacecraft reach outer space

THERMOSPHERE
• 80–450 km (50–280 miles)
• reaches 2,000°C (3,632°F)
• contains the ionosphere – electrically-charged air that reflects radio waves

MESOSPHERE
• 50–80 km (30–50 miles)
• meteors burn up and cause shooting stars

STRATOSPHERE
• 20–50 km (12–30 miles)
• ranges from –60°C (–76°F) to just about freezing point at the top
• calm layer where airliners fly
• contains the ozone layer that protects us from the Sun's harmful rays

TROPOSPHERE
• up to 20 km (12 miles) above the Earth
• weather layer, where rain clouds form

THE OXYGEN CYCLE

A vast store of oxygen exists in oceans, rocks, and the atmosphere. Oxygen created by plant photosynthesis balances oxygen used up when animals breathe.

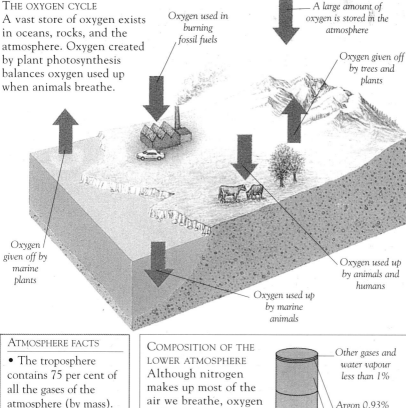

Oxygen used in burning fossil fuels

A large amount of oxygen is stored in the atmosphere

Oxygen given off by trees and plants

Oxygen given off by marine plants

Oxygen used up by animals and humans

Oxygen used up by marine animals

ATMOSPHERE FACTS

• The troposphere contains 75 per cent of all the gases of the atmosphere (by mass).

• Ozone is a type of oxygen that absorbs damaging ultraviolet rays from the Sun.

• Humans can only live and breathe normally in the troposphere layer.

COMPOSITION OF THE LOWER ATMOSPHERE

Although nitrogen makes up most of the air we breathe, oxygen is the essential gas for all animal and human life. Nitrogen is simply breathed in and out. Other gases, such as argon and carbon dioxide, make up less than one per cent.

Other gases and water vapour less than 1%

Argon 0.93%

Oxygen 21%

Nitrogen 78%

MAPPING THE EARTH

MAPS HELP US TO see what the Earth looks like. A map uses symbols to represent different features of the Earth. A technique called projection can transfer the curved surface of the globe on to a flat sheet of paper. Aerial photographs help make maps that show valleys and hills. On a larger scale, satellite photographs help map-makers reveal how the Earth looks from space.

The Arctic circle is measured at 66°32' from North.

GEOGRAPHIC NORTH POLE

Line of longitude

Tropic of Cancer

The equator

Tropic of Capricorn

Line of latitude

EARTH'S GRID
Imaginary lines of longitude and latitude form a grid on the Earth. The grid is used to aid navigation.

Satellite takes thousands of photographs

Lines of longitude run between the north and south poles, and lines of latitude are parallel to the equator.

GEOGRAPHIC SOUTH POLE

Area of the Earth's surface photographed

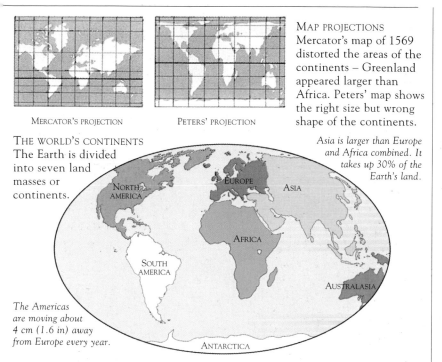

MERCATOR'S PROJECTION

PETERS' PROJECTION

MAP PROJECTIONS
Mercator's map of 1569 distorted the areas of the continents – Greenland appeared larger than Africa. Peters' map shows the right size but wrong shape of the continents.

THE WORLD'S CONTINENTS
The Earth is divided into seven land masses or continents.

NORTH AMERICA

EUROPE

ASIA

AFRICA

SOUTH AMERICA

AUSTRALASIA

ANTARCTICA

Asia is larger than Europe and Africa combined. It takes up 30% of the Earth's land.

The Americas are moving about 4 cm (1.6 in) away from Europe every year.

SATELLITE MAPPING
While orbiting the Earth, satellites photograph the planet in sections. The separate images are combined to give a clear picture of the Earth.

Satellite's orbit around the poles

Direction of the Earth's rotation

THE SIZE OF THE CONTINENTS

CONTINENT	AREA IN SQ KM	AREA IN SQ MILES
Asia	44,485,900	17,176,100
Africa	30, 269,680	11,687,180
North America	24,235,280	9,357,290
South America	17,820,770	6,880,630
Antarctica	13,209,000	5,100,020
Europe	10,530,750	4,065,940
Australasia	7,682,300	2,966,368

EARTH'S PLATES AND CONTINENTS

THE EARTH'S CRUST

EARTH'S SURFACE IS covered by a thin layer of rock called crust. Rocky crust above sea level forms islands and continents. The crust, or lithosphere, is in pieces, or plates, that move slowly all the time. Where two plates meet they may slide past each other or one may go under another. New crust forms under the ocean while old crust slips beneath plates.

PLATE FACTS

• Earth's plates "float" on a slushy layer called the asthenosphere.

• The size of the Earth doesn't change – new crust produced equals older crust consumed.

EARTH'S SKIN
Earth's crust, like the skin of an apple, is a thin covering for what is inside. Under the ocean the crust, called oceanic crust, is 6 km (4 miles) thick, but under mountain ranges the continental crust can be 64 km (40 miles) thick.

The rock plates of the Earth's crust fit together like pieces of a jigsaw

CROSS-SECTION THROUGH THE EARTH'S CRUST
This section through the Earth's crust at the Equator shows the landscape and the direction of plate movement at plate boundaries.

AFRICA

African Rift Valley

INDIAN OCEAN

Indo-Australian plate

African plate

African plate

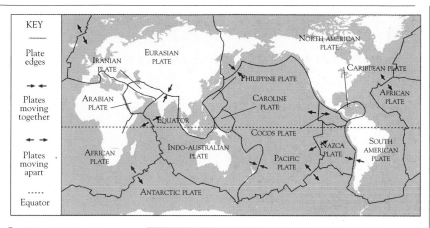

KEY

— Plate edges

→ ← Plates moving together

← → Plates moving apart

..... Equator

NORTH AMERICAN PLATE
EURASIAN PLATE
IRANIAN PLATE
PHILIPPINE PLATE
CARIBBEAN PLATE
ARABIAN PLATE
CAROLINE PLATE
AFRICAN PLATE
EQUATOR
COCOS PLATE
SOUTH AMERICAN PLATE
AFRICAN PLATE
INDO-AUSTRALIAN PLATE
NAZCA PLATE
PACIFIC PLATE
ANTARCTIC PLATE

PLATES OF THE WORLD
The surface of the Earth has 15 large plates. A plate can include both continental lithosphere and oceanic lithosphere. Areas such as Australia lie in the middle of a plate, while others, like Iceland, have a plate boundary through them.

MOVEMENT OF THE EARTH'S PLATES

PLATE NAMES	DIRECTION OF MOVEMENT	RATE OF MOVEMENT	
		CM PER YEAR	IN PER YEAR
Pacific/Nazca	apart	18.3	7.3
Cocos/Pacific	apart	11.7	4.6
Nazca/South American	together	11.2	4.4
Pacific/Indo-Australian	together	10.5	4.1
Pacific/Antarctic	apart	10.3	4.0

Sunda trench

Indo-Australian plate

INDONESIA

There is no relative motion between these plates

PACIFIC OCEAN

Eurasian plate

Caroline plate

Pacific plate

MOVING CONTINENTS

EARTH'S CONTINENTS can be rearranged to fit together like pieces of a jigsaw. This idea made scientists think that they once formed a giant landmass, Pangaea. This "supercontinent" broke up, and the continents drifted, over millions of years, to where they are now. This is continental drift or plate tectonics theory. Continents move as the Earth's plates move, sliding along on the asthenosphere, a layer of soft mantle.

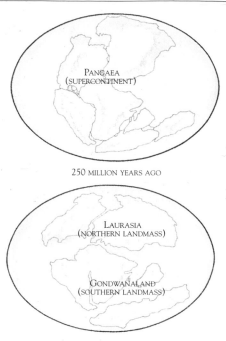

250 MILLION YEARS AGO

120 MILLION YEARS AGO

CONTINENTAL DRIFT
When Pangaea broke up, new continents emerged. The outlines of South America and Africa appeared.

CROSS-SECTION THROUGH THE EARTH'S CRUST   PACIFIC OCEAN

Pacific plate   *Nazca plat*

PLATE BOUNDARIES

Volcanoes at subduction zone

Mid-ocean ridge

Subduction zone

Transform fault

WHERE PLATES MEET

At a transform fault, plates slide past one another. A subduction zone is where two plates collide. One plate is forced into the mantle and molten rock material rises to form volcanoes. At a mid-ocean ridge new crust rises between plates.

PUSH THEORY

Heat inside the Earth forces the mantle to rise. It erupts at mid-ocean ridges, pushing plates apart.

PULL THEORY

Rising molten rock cools and solidifies. This denser rock sinks at trenches and gravity pulls the plate down.

Andes

Amazon Basin

Mid-Atlantic Ridge

SOUTH AMERICA

ATLANTIC OCEAN

American plate

African plate

MOVING CONTINENTS

25

INSIDE THE EARTH

THE INTERIOR OF the Earth has four major layers. On the outside is the crust made of familiar soil and rock. Under this is the mantle, which is solid rock with a molten layer at the top. The inside or core of the Earth has two sections: an outer core of thick fluid, and a solid inner core.

The atmosphere stretches about 640 km (400 miles) into space

The crust varies between about 6 and 64 km (4 and 40 miles) thick

The mantle is 2,900 km (1,800 miles) thick

The outer core is 2,000 km (1,240 miles) thick

The inner core is 2,740 km (1,700 miles) thick

LAYERS OF THE EARTH
Earth's outer shell is called the lithosphere. It includes the crust and part of the upper mantle. The crust floats on the asthenosphere, like an iceberg on the sea. Earth's outer core is mostly oxygen, liquid iron, and nickel. Its inner core, about 4,000°C (7,232°F), is solid iron and nickel.

Mount Everest reaches up 8.85 km (5.5 miles)

A deep coal mine reaches down less than 1 km (0.62 miles) below sea level

The deepest mine reaches down 3.8 km (2.34 miles)

The deepest hole has reached 12 km (7.5 miles)

Sea level

The deepest ocean drilling has reached 1.7 km (1.05 miles)

CRUST

MANTLE

UNDER THE CRUST

Clues to the interior of the Earth come from boreholes. These have only reached as far as the crust. They reveal a dense lower layer and a less dense upper layer to the crust. There is also evidence of a boundary between crust and mantle called the Moho.

CRUST FACTS

• If an excavator could dig a hole through the Earth at 1 m (39 in) per minute, it would take 24 years to reach the other side.

• Western Deep Gold Mine in South Africa is the world's deepest mine. It is 3.8 km (2.36 miles) deep.

• The Earth's crust is mainly granite rock.

COMPOSTION OF THE EARTH'S CRUST

Light elements such as silicon, oxygen, and aluminium make up the Earth's crust. Oceanic crust is mostly basalt (which also contains magnesium and iron). Continental crust is composed of granite-like rocks. These may have been formed from recycled basaltic ocean crust.

Other elements 2%
Potassium 2.6%
Magnesium 2%
Sodium 2.8%
Iron 5%
Aluminium 8%
Calcium 3.6%
Silicon 28%
Oxygen 46%

VOLCANOES

EXTINCT VOLCANO
Castle Rock, Edinburgh is an extinct volcano. It has not erupted for 340 million years. An extinct volcano such as this is not expected to erupt again.

DORMANT VOLCANO
If scientists believe a volcano may erupt again, perhaps because it gives off volcanic gases, it is called dormant. Mt. Rainier, U.S.A. is described as dormant.

THE EARTH'S VOLCANOES

MOST VOLCANOES are found near the coast or under the ocean. They usually form at plate edges. Here crust movement allows hot molten rock called magma to rise up from inside the Earth and burst through the crust. Hot magma is called lava when it flows out of a volcano. Ash, steam, and gas also spew out and cause great destruction.

COMPARING ERUPTIONS
One way to compare the size of different volcanic eruptions is to measure the amount of ash thrown out during an eruption.

MT. ST. HELENS, U.S.A. 1980
1 KM³
(0.24 MILES³)

MT. VESUVIUS, ITALY, A.D. 79
3 KM³
(0.72 MILES³)

MT. KATMAI, U.S.A., 1912
12 KM³
(2.88 MILES³)

MT. KRAKATOA, INDONESIA, 1883
18 KM³
(4.32 MILES³)

MT. TAMBORA, INDONESIA, 1815
80 KM³
(19.2 MILES³)

VOLCANO SITES

In general, volcanoes, like earthquakes, occur near plate boundaries. Plate destruction (around the Pacific Ocean) and plate construction (in Hawaii) cause volcanoes.

The chain of volcanoes around the edge of the Pacific Ocean is known as the "Ring of Fire".

Ring of Fire continues through volcanic islands of Japan

PACIFIC OCEAN

POMPEII

In A.D 79 Mt. Vesuvius erupted burying the town of Pompeii under pumice and ash. The two-day eruption killed 2,000 people with poisonous gases and hot ash.

LARGEST VOLCANIC EXPLOSIONS

The Volcanic Explosivity Index (V.E.I.) grades eruptions from 0 to 8. The scale is based on the height of the dust cloud, the volume of tephra (debris ejected by a volcano), and an account of the severity of the eruption. Any eruption above 5 on the scale is very large and violent. So far, there has never been an eruption of 8.

VOLCANO	DATE	V.E.I.
Crater Lake, Oregon, U.S.A.	c.4895B.C.	7
Towada, Honshu, Japan	915	5
Oraefajokull, Iceland	1362	6
Tambora, Indonesia	1815	7
Krakatoa, Indonesia	1883	6
Santa Maria, Guatemala	1902	6
Mt. Katmai, Alaska	1912	6
Mt. St. Helens, U.S.A.	1980	5

31

VOLCANO SHAPES

NOT ALL VOLCANOES are the same. Some are cone-shaped and others are quite flat. The shape of the volcano depends on the kind of lava that comes out of it. Runny lava flows away from the volcano before hardening, but thick, viscous lava forms a hard cone. Volcanoes usually appear near plate boundaries, but they also form at hot spots such as in Hawaii or under the ocean at plate edges.

ICELAND'S RIFT
Skaftar fissure in Iceland lies where two plates are moving apart. It is part of a 27-km (16-mile) rift along the plates' edges.

VOLCANO FACTS

• Kilauea, Hawaii is the most frequently active volcano.

• There are known to be about 1,300 active volcanoes in the world.

Crack in the Earth's crust

Main vent

Side vent

Vent

Lava

FISSURE VOLCANO
This type of volcano is a long crack in the crust. Runny lava seeps out along its length and forms a plateau.

SHIELD VOLCANO
A shield volcano usually has several side vents. The lava is runny and produces gently sloping sides.

WORST VOLCANIC ERUPTIONS		
VOLCANO	DATE	NUMBER KILLED
Tambora	1815	92,000
Mt. Pelée	1902	40,000
Krakatoa	1883	36,000
Nevado del Ruiz	1985	23,000

COMPOSITE VOLCANO
Cone-shaped volcanoes build up from sticky lava. Inside are layers of thick lava and ash from previous eruptions. Gas builds pressure inside the volcano so that it erupts violently.

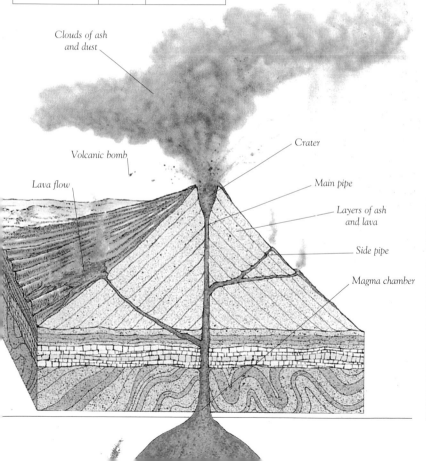

Clouds of ash and dust

Volcanic bomb

Lava flow

Crater

Main pipe

Layers of ash and lava

Side pipe

Magma chamber

33

EXPLOSIVE VOLCANOES

SOMETIMES VOLCANOES explode violently. Volcanoes that form from viscous lava are most likely to do this.

NUÉE ARDENTE
An explosive eruption can cause a glowing ash cloud or *nuée ardente*.

The thick, sticky lava traps gas under it and plugs the volcano's vent. When pressure increases, a violent explosion blows out the lava. Pieces of rock and a great deal of ash are hurled high into the air. Clouds of ash and pumice flow like hot avalanches down the sides of the volcano. Mudflows (also called lahars) are a mixture of water and ash. They travel at great speed and engulf everything in their paths.

BEFORE MT. ST. HELENS ERUPTED

MT. ST. HELENS
In the Cascades, U.S.A. a peaceful-looking volcano erupted after 123 years of dormancy. A warning came when one side of the volcano began to bulge as the magma rose. A gas explosion lasting 9 hours and a landslide ensued. An ash cloud over 1,500 km² (580 miles²) caused darkness. Melted snow and ash made mudflows.

ERUPTION ON 18TH MAY 1980

PUMICE FACTS

- Pumice is really light-weight frothed glass that is able to float on water.

- Pumice is used in industry as an abrasive for soft metals. It is also used for insulation in some buildings.

DEVASTATING MUDFLOWS

When Ruiz volcano in Colombia erupted in 1985, the snow melted around its summit. A mixture of water, ash, and pumice fast turned to mud and buried the nearby city of Armero. More than 22,000 people were drowned in the mud.

PRODUCTS OF EXPLOSIVE VOLCANOES

ASH
Particles of lava fall like ash and cover the land.

LAPILLI
Lava ejected in pea-sized pieces is called lapilli.

PUMICE
Pumice is light-weight lava filled with holes.

BOMB
Bomb-shaped lava forms as it flies in the air.

PELE'S HAIR
Sometimes drops of liquid lava blow into fine spiky strands. The threads form needles of volcanic glass. They are named Pele's hair after Pele, the Hawaiian goddess of volcanoes.

NON-EXPLOSIVE VOLCANOES

SOME VOLCANOES ARE cracks in the ground oozing runny lava. This type of lava flows for long distances before it cools. It builds low-sided volcanoes and plateaus of lava. This kind of volcano forms at plate edges, mostly under the ocean. A hot spot volcano bursts through the middle of a plate; it is not related to plate margins.

SPREADING RIDGES
The boundary where two plates are moving apart is usually underwater. In some places, such as Iceland, the spreading ridge is above sea level. Magma rises along this boundary and lava erupts. The lava may form mountains at the spreading ridge.

TYPES OF LAVA

PAHOEHOE LAVA
Lava with a wrinkled skin is called pahoehoe. This is a nonviscous or runny lava that forms a skin as it cools, although the inside is still molten. It is common in Hawaii.

AA LAVA
This is the Hawaiian name for slow-moving, sticky, viscous lava. When aa lava solidifies it has a rough, jagged surface that is also described as blocky.

HAWAIIAN VOLCANOES
At places called hot spots, notably in Hawaii, magma rises to create fire fountains and fire curtains.

HOT SPOT VOLCANOES
The Earth's plates move slowly over hot spots in the crust. Magma rises, punching through the crust to form a new island. In Hawaii, a hot spot has built a chain of volcanic islands.

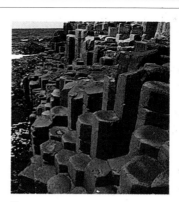

BASALT COLUMNS
Northern Ireland's Giant's Causeway is made of mostly hexagonal columns of basalt rock. At least 60 million years ago, thick lava cooled and shrank to form the blocks.

CHAIN OF HAWAIIAN ISLANDS

KAUAI

OAHU

MAUI

HAWAII

Volcanic island no longer above hot spot.

Plate moves over the hot spot, while the hot spot remains stationary.

The hot spot is now south of Hawaii, where a new volcano is growing under the sea

OLD FAITHFUL
This geyser called Old
Faithful is in the U.S.A.
It shoots out a column of
boiling water and steam
every hour and has done
so for the last 100 years.

VOLCANIC LANDSCAPES

MOVEMENT IN ROCKS underground can cause changes to the landscape above. The combination of heat and water in the Earth's rocks produces various phenomena. Molten rock erupting out of the Earth brings gases, mineral deposits, and water with it. Mud pools, hot springs, and geysers form when the gases and water escape. Chemical reactions also occur, changing rocks and depositing minerals in the water near them.

THE LANDSCAPE AROUND VOLCANOES

Steaming hot water

Volcanic gases bubble through liquid mud

HOT SPRINGS
Magma heats water stored in cracks in rock. The water returns to the surface as a hot spring.

MUD POOLS
Volcanic gases dissolve rock. Particles of rock mix with water to form bubbling mud pools.

FUMAROLES
As magma rises, it cools and gives off gases. Small holes or fumaroles in the rock let the gases escape.

PILLOW LAVA

When lava erupts underwater at spreading ridges, it can produce these rounded shapes called pillow lava. The sea water cools the lava rapidly, so that as it solidifies a crust forms around each lump. The lava formed is typically an igneous rock called basalt.

A NEW ISLAND

In 1963, off the Icelandic coast, a new island rose up from under the sea. Volcanic activity underwater brought magma to the surface. Sea water and hot magma produced explosions and huge amounts of steam. Now, plants grow in the fertile soil.

GEYSERS

Magma inside the Earth heats water in the rocks. The water shoots from the ground as steam jets.

TERRACES

Hot water stored in rock can dissolve minerals. Minerals are deposited in terraces around a vent.

GEYSER FACTS

• The tallest geyser is Yellowstone National Park's Steamboat Geyser in Wyoming, U.S.A. It reaches 60–115 m (195–380 ft).

• Strokkur Geyser in Iceland spurts every 10 to 15 minutes.

• In 1904, Waimangu Geyser, New Zealand erupted to a height of 460 m (1,500 ft).

EARTHQUAKES

WHEN THE EARTH SHAKES

MORE THAN A million times a year, the Earth's crust suddenly shakes during an earthquake. Most of the world's earthquakes are fairly slight. A mild earthquake can feel like a truck passing; a severe one can destroy roads and buildings and cause the sea to rise in huge waves. Earthquakes often happen near volcanoes and young mountain ranges: at the edges of the Earth's plates.

A SEVERE EARTHQUAKE
San Francisco, U.S.A. was shaken by a devastating earthquake in 1906. Only the chimney stacks were left standing.

Surface waves radiate from the epicentre

The focus is inside the Earth

Shock waves go through the Earth and up to the surface

CENTRE OF AN EARTHQUAKE
The earthquake is strongest at the focus. At the epicentre, the point on the surface above the focus, the crust shakes and sends out shock waves. The waves bend as they travel through layers of rock in the Earth.

EARTHQUAKE FAULT ZONES

Earthquakes occur at cracks in the crust called faults. Deep earthquakes take place where one plate is sliding under another.

Many earthquakes occur on the north-east coast of Asia. This is at the boundary of two of the Earth's plates

Stress builds up in rocks along the fault line

BEFORE AN EARTHQUAKE

AFTER AN EARTHQUAKE

The plates slip into a new position

SLIDING PLATES

Earthquakes occur at spreading ridges, subduction zones, and transform faults, where two plates slide past each other. Stress builds up in rock and causes a sudden movement as the rock jolts into a new position. Foreshocks may precede an earthquake, and aftershocks follow it.

EARTHQUAKE FACTS

• Before an earthquake it is reported that dogs howl, pandas moan, and well water bubbles.

• A strong earthquake can cause the ground to roll like waves at sea.

• The 1755 earthquake in Lisbon, Portugal lasted ten minutes. It was felt as far away as north Africa.

• About 90 per cent of earthquakes occur in the Ring of Fire around the Pacific Ocean.

EARTHQUAKE DESTRUCTION
In 1994, an earthquake caused
devastation in Los Angeles, U.S.A.
Roads and buildings collapsed,
water mains and gas pipes burst,
and fires began in the city. Many
buildings in Los Angeles were built
to be earthquake-proof and so did
not suffer very much damage.
The earthquake measured 5.7
on the Richter scale.

MEASURING EARTHQUAKES

SCIENTISTS WHO STUDY
earthquakes are known as
seismologists (*seismos* is the
Greek word for earthquakes).
Seismologists monitor the
vibrations or shock waves
that pass through the Earth
using an instrument called
a seismometer. Predicting
earthquakes is very difficult.
Scientists look for warnings
such as bulges in the ground
or cracks in surface rocks.

MERCALLI SCALE
Giuseppe Mercalli
(1850–1914) devised
a method of grading
earthquakes based on
the observation of their
effects. Using this scale
enables the amount of
shaking, or intensity, of
different earthquakes
to be easily compared.
On Mercalli's scale
earthquakes are graded
from 1 to 12.

1 • detected by instruments
2 • felt by people resting
3 • hanging light bulbs sway
4 • felt by people indoors
  • plates, windows rattle
  • parked cars rock

5 • buildings tremble
  • felt by most people
  • liquids spill
6 • movement felt by all
  • pictures fall off wall
  • windows break

SEISMOMETER

This device records how much the Earth shakes during an earthquake. A weight keeps the pen still while the machine holding it moves with the Earth.

RICHTER SCALE

The amount of energy released by an earthquake can be measured on the Richter scale. An increase of 1.0 on the scale represents a tenfold increase in energy.

EARTHQUAKE	DATE	RICHTER SCALE
North Peru	1970	7.7
Mexico City	1985	7.8
Erzincan	1939	7.9
Tangshan	1976	8.0
Tokyo	1923	8.3
Kansu	1920	8.6

A pen records the movement on a rotating drum.

Base moves with the horizontal motion of the Earth.

The reading from a seismometer is called a seismogram. It indicates the extent of the Earth's shaking, either up and down or from side to side.

7 • bricks and tiles fall
  • chimneys crack
  • difficult to stand
8 • steering cars difficult
  • tree branches snap
  • chimneys fall

9 • ground cracks
  • mud oozes from ground
  • general panic
10 • underground pipes burst
  • river water spills out
  • most buildings collapse

11 • bridges collapse
  • railway lines buckle
  • landslides occur
12 • near total destruction
  • rivers change course
  • waves seen on ground

EARTHQUAKE DAMAGE

IN GENERAL, great loss of life during an earthquake can be avoided. It is often not the Earth's shaking that kills people but falling buildings, particularly poorly constructed ones. Earthquakes can trigger landslides and tsunamis which can be destructive. During an earthquake it is best to stay indoors under a sturdy table. Outdoors, falling masonry is a hazard.

ESTIMATED LIVES LOST AS A RESULT OF RECENT EARTHQUAKES		
PLACE	YEAR	ESTIMATED DEATHS
Tangshan, China	1976	695,000
Kansu, China	1920	100,000
Tokyo, Japan	1976	99,000
Messina, Italy	1908	80,000
Armenia	1988	55,000
North-west Iran	1990	40,000
Erzincan, Turkey	1939	30,000

FIRE HAZARD
Fire poses a great danger following an earthquake. Gas leaks and petrol spills can lead to large fires like this in San Francisco, U.S.A. in 1989.

JAPANESE PRINT SHOWING
A TSUNAMI TALLER THAN
MT. FUJI IN JAPAN.

TSUNAMIS

An earthquake just off the coast can start a wave motion at sea. In the ocean the wave is low but as it nears the shore the front of it slows and water behind builds up to form a huge tsumani.

TSUNAMI FACTS

• The highest tsunami wave was 85 m (279 ft) high. It struck Ishigaki Island, Japan in 1971.

• In the open ocean, a tsunami can travel at speeds of up to 600 km (373 miles) per hour.

LANDSLIDES

Loose rock and debris may be dislodged by an earthquake and cause landslides as here in Alaska in 1964. Avalanches too may be triggered by the ground shaking. Mudflows or lahars can result from rain or snow mixing with loosened soil.

EARTHQUAKE-PROOF BUILDINGS

A great deal of damage is caused by buildings collapsing during earthquakes. In earthquake-prone San Francisco and Japan there are safety guidelines that all new buildings must meet. Wooden buildings are replaced with concrete and concrete and steel foundations are used.

Pyramid-shaped buildings are built to withstand stress

The central column of the pagoda absorbs the shaking

TRANSAMERICA
BUILDING, SAN FRANCISCO

ANCIENT BUDDHIST
PAGODA, JAPAN

EARTHQUAKE DAMAGE

LANDSCAPE, WEATHERING, AND EROSION

LANDSCAPES AND SOIL

THE WEATHER'S EFFECT on rock is what produces soil. This complex process takes many thousands of years. Climate, vegetation, and rock type determine what type of soil forms. As well as rock, soil contains organic matter from decaying plants and animals (humus). Soil covers the landscape and is a medium for plants to grow in.

PEAT LANDSCAPE
This landscape is green and low-lying. Spongy peat soil is rich in humus from decayed bog plants. It retains water and nutrients easily.

SANDY LANDSCAPE
In arid (dry) sandy landscapes there is little vegetation. The soil contains hardly any organic material. Winds blow away small particles leaving sand and stones.

TYPES OF SOIL
Chalky soil is thin and stony; water passes through it quickly. Water drains easily through sandy soil, washing out nutrients. Clay soil retains nutrients and moisture but is difficult for plants to take root in. Peat soil is acidic. It holds water and minerals.

CLAY

SAND

PEAT

CHALK

SOIL FACTS

- 1 m³ (10.8 ft³) of soil may contain more than 1,000 million animals.

- Some soils in India, Africa, and Australia are 2 million years old.

- It takes about 500 years for 2.5 cm (1 in) of topsoil to form.

SOIL PROFILE

A slice of soil down to the bedrock is called a soil profile. The profile shows several layers, or horizons. The number and thickness of horizons vary with the soil type.

HORIZON 0
- humus layer
- contains live and decaying plants and soil animals

HORIZON A
- topsoil
- dark and fertile
- rich in humus

HORIZON B
- subsoil
- contains minerals washed down from topsoil
- little organic matter

HORIZON C
- infertile layer
- composed of weathered parent rock

HORIZON D
- bedrock (parent rock)
- source of soil's minerals

SOIL CREEP AND EROSION

Gravity and water pull soil down a slope particle by particle. This is called soil creep. Plant roots bind soil and help to prevent it from wearing away, or eroding. Overgrazing and felling forests both lead to soil erosion.

Trees will curve to grow upward towards the light

Soil creep is indicated by leaning structures such as walls and telegraph poles

Cracks appear in roads as the soil under them moves downhill

EROSION IN WET CLIMATES

AS SOON AS ROCK is exposed on the Earth's surface, it is attacked by wind, water, or ice – a process known as

weathering. This prepares for erosion, when rock is broken down and removed. Weathering can be either physical (wearing away the rock itself) or chemical (attacking the minerals in the rock). Climate and rock type determine the kind of weathering that occurs. In wet climates chemical weathering, mainly by rainwater, is dominant.

MOUNTAIN STREAM
Cascading over steep gradients, a swift-flowing stream wears away softer rocks. Harder rocks remain and create rocky outcrops. These become steep rapids or waterfalls where the water tumbles downhill.

TREE-ROOT ACTION
As trees and other plants grow, their roots push down into small cracks in the rock. The cracks widen as the roots grow and eventually the rock breaks up.

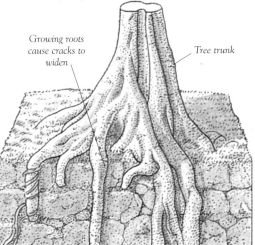

Growing roots cause cracks to widen

Tree trunk

FROST SHATTERING

This type of weathering occurs when water in cracks in the rock freezes and expands. Joints in the rock widen and the rock shatters.

Fragments of fallen rock, called scree, collect at the base of a slope

Shattering leaves sharp broken edges on the rock's surface

EROSION FACTS

• Acid rain can dissolve rock as deep as 30 m (98 ft) below the surface.

• Erosion is fastest in steep, rainy areas and semi-arid areas with little vegetation.

• The rate of erosion for the whole of the world's land area is estimated to be 8.6 cm (3.3 in) every 1,000 years.

CLINTS AND GRIKES

Acid in rainwater seeps into limestone joints and dissolves the calcite in the rock. Ridges known as clints and grooves known as grikes form in the rock.

ACID RAIN

Rainwater naturally contains a weak acid called carbonic acid. However, the burning of fossil fuels produces gases such as sulphur dioxide. When this combines with rainwater it produces sulphuric acid – an ingredient of "acid rain". Acid rain damages trees and lake life.

Acid rain slowly dissolves rocks such as limestone and marble

LIMESTONE STATUES SUFFER EROSION BY ACID RAIN

EROSION IN ARID CLIMATES

IN HOT, DRY, DESERT areas extremes of temperature cause rocks to fragment. By day rock expands in the heat and by night it contracts in the cold. It is mainly physical weathering that occurs in arid climates, chiefly caused by wind. The sand-filled wind blasts rocks and builds shifting sand dunes.

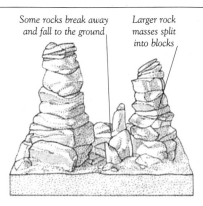

Some rocks break away and fall to the ground

Larger rock masses split into blocks

BLOCK DISINTEGRATION
Acute temperature changes can cause rocks to break up. Joints in the rock grow wider with the rock's cycle of expansion and contraction. Large pieces split into small blocks.

ONION-SKIN LAYERING
In the heat of the desert, a rock's surface may expand though the interior stays cool. At night, the surface of the rock cools and contracts. This daily process causes flaking on the surface of the rock, and the outer layers begin to peel and fall away.

SAND DUNES

Direction of wind

Eddies build where the wind slows

LINEAR OR SEIF DUNE
This type of dune has long parallel ridges. It forms where the wind blows continually in one direction.

ZEUGENS

Sand carried by the wind sculpts these strange forms called zeugens. Sand wears away soft rock leaving behind areas of harder rock, worn into jagged shapes.

Most erosion occurs up to 1 m (3.3 ft) from the ground

Sand bounced along by the wind

Top-heavy shapes result from the erosion

MUSHROOM ROCKS

The desert wind contains a great deal of sand which scours away the surface of rocks. Mushroom-shaped rocks are a result of this action. Rocks are worn away most at their base by the sand, leaving behind a landscape of rock pedestals.

SECTION THROUGH A BARKHAN DUNE

Sand slips down the face of the dune

Sand builds up in the centre of the dune

A strong wind blows across the top of the dune

Weak wind at the base of the dune

BARKHAN DUNE

A sand dune with a crescent-shaped front and a long, sloping tail is called a barkhan dune. This is the most common dune shape in sandy deserts.

SAND DUNE FACTS

• Sand is composed mostly of the hard mineral quartz.

• Linear or seif dunes can reach 215 m (700 ft) high.

• Not all dunes are made of sand – dunes can form from salt crystals, gypsum, or shell fragments.

• Black sand dunes form in volcanic areas.

ROCKS AND MINERALS

IGNEOUS ROCKS

"FIERY" OR IGNEOUS rocks such as granite and basalt originate from molten magma. The magma is produced deep inside the Earth where rocks melt in the heat of the mantle and crust. Magma that cools and solidifies under the Earth's surface forms intrusive igneous rock. If it erupts as lava from a volcano and then cools on the surface of the Earth, it is known as extrusive igneous rock.

INTRUSIVE IGNEOUS ROCK
Sugar Loaf Mountain, Brazil formed from magma that solidified underground. Eventually, the surrounding rock eroded leaving this dome shape.

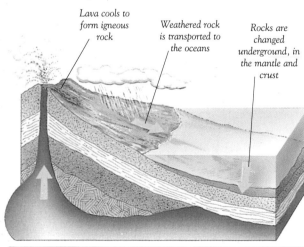

Lava cools to form igneous rock

Weathered rock is transported to the oceans

Rocks are changed underground, in the mantle and crust

THE ROCK CYCLE
Rocks constantly pass through a recycling process. Crustal movements bring igneous rocks to the surface. The rocks weather away and the particles build sedimentary rocks. Pressure and heat underground may change, or metamorphose, rocks before they re-emerge.

SYDNEY HARBOUR BRIDGE

The supporting pylons of this famous bridge in Sydney, Australia are built from granite. The span of the bridge is 503 m (1,650 ft) and the arch is made of steel. Granite is often used as a building material because of its strength and availability.

IGNEOUS ROCK FACTS

- Basalt makes up most of the ocean floor.

- Obsidian was used in early jewellery and tools.

- Most continental igneous rocks are quartz, feldspar, and mica.

- Earth's first rocks were igneous rocks.

TYPES OF IGNEOUS ROCK

Shell-like, curved fracture

OBSIDIAN
This lava forms a natural glass. Its smooth texture is due to rapid cooling.

Granite has coarse grains

GABBRO
This intrusive, coarse-grained rock forms from slow-cooled lava.

BASALT
From runny lava that flows great distances, basalt is fine-grained.

PINK GRANITE
Granite is a common intrusive rock. Crystals of pink feldspar, black mica, and grey quartz minerals are visible.

IGNEOUS ROCKS

59

SEDIMENTARY ROCKS

ROCK IS GRADUALLY weakened by the weather. Particles of rock are then carried off by rain or wind. These particles build up into layers of sediment. Sediment combines with plant and animal debris and hardens. Water in the ground can help to cement the sediment and turn it into rock (a process known as lithification). By studying sedimentary rock layers, scientists can uncover the environment of the past.

STRATA
Over millions of years, layers of sediment are pressed into bands of rock called strata. Strata in the Grand Canyon, U.S.A. preserve a record of the region's history.

FLINT TOOLS
Prehistoric people fashioned tools from a sedimentary rock called flint. Flint was chipped into shape using a stone. It is a common rock that flakes easily, leaving a sharp edge. Prehistoric tools such as hand axes and adzes (for shaping wood) have been found.

FLINT ADZE

CHALK CLIFFS
These cliffs in Sussex, England are a type of limestone. They are calcium carbonate (chalk) and contain fossils of micro-organisms.

EGYPTIAN PYRAMIDS AT GIZA
Elaborate tombs (begun c.2686 B.C.) for the Egyptian pharaohs, were constructed at Giza, Egypt. They were built from nummulitic limestone which contains many large marine fossils called *nummulites*.

TYPES OF SEDIMENTARY ROCK

BRECCIA
Fragments of rock cemented together make up breccia.

CHALK
Skeletons of tiny sea animals form this type of limestone. Chalk is fine-grained and soft.

RED SANDSTONE
Cemented sand grains coated with iron oxide make up this sedimentary rock.

SHELLY LIMESTONE
This rock contains a great many fossils cemented together with calcite. Limestone usually forms in a shallow sea, though it can come from a freshwater environment. It is possible to find the source of a specimen by studying the fossils it contains.

FOSSILS

PLANTS AND ANIMALS that lived millions of years ago are preserved in rocks as fossils. A fossil is the remains of an organism, a cast of an animal or plant made from minerals, or even burrows or tracks left by animals and preserved in rock. Sedimentary rocks such as limestone or chalk hold fossils. Palaeontologists are scientists who study fossils.

PLANT FOSSIL
Seed ferns like this one were widespread in the hot swamps of the late Carboniferous period. These primitive land plants, with some adaptations, still exist today.

THE FOSSILIZATION PROCESS

1 When an animal or plant dies underwater, it falls to the seabed. The soft parts of its body decay or are eaten by animals.

2 The organism is buried in layers of sediment. Hard parts of the animal, such as the shell, bones, or teeth, are preserved.

3 Minerals in the seabed react with the shell to harden it. Some animals decay, leaving a space where a cast forms.

INSECT FOSSIL
Early dragonflies preserved in limestone have been found in Europe and Australasia. This one dates from the Jurassic period.

DRAGONFLY (PETALURA)

FISH FOSSIL
Fish are the most primitive vertebrates (animals with backbones). This fish first appeared 30 to 24.5 million years ago, long after the dinosaurs had died out.

SEED FERN (ALETHOPTERIS)

FISH FROM THE OLIGOCENE PERIOD

4 Further sediments cover the fossil. Uplift or erosion of the crust may eventually expose the fossil at the surface.

TRACE FOSSILS
Fossilized droppings or tracks are called trace fossils. This dinosaur footprint was left in mud 135 million years ago.

FOSSIL FACTS

• The earliest dinosaur, a *Herrerasaurus*, was found in Argentina in 1989 and dated at 230 million years old.

• The largest fossil footprint was left by a hadrosaurid. It is 1.36 m (4.46 ft) long.

• Fossils of cells are the first evidence of life, 3,200 million years ago.

63

THE AGES OF THE EARTH

THE EARTH'S HISTORY divides into eras, periods, and epochs. The timescale is marked by the appearance of new lifeforms. Life on Earth is never static – it changes and evolves constantly. Creatures become extinct and others appear. Some creatures may be short-lived and others survive unchanged for millions of years. Using fossil evidence scientists build a picture of life in the past.

JELLYFISH FOSSIL

PRECAMBRIAN FOSSIL
This fossil is about 570 million years old. It is a kind of primitive jellyfish that lived in Australia.

MORE FOSSIL FACTS

• Our species, *Homo sapiens*, first appeared about 40,000 years ago.

• A million Ice Age fossils were found preserved in the tar pits of La Brea, U.S.A.

CARBONIFEROUS SWAMP
Extensive swamps covered the land during the Carboniferous period (363–290 million years ago). It was during this time that forests, containing seed plants and ferns, flourished. Some of these were preserved and now form coal deposits. The first reptiles and giant dragonflies lived in these swamps.

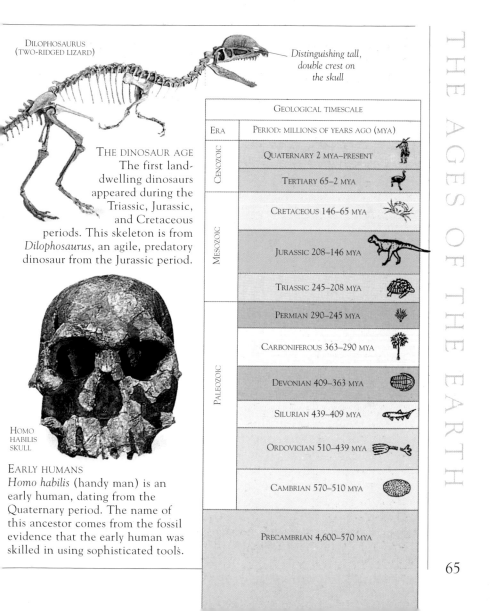

DILOPHOSAURUS
(TWO-RIDGED LIZARD)

*Distinguishing tall,
double crest on
the skull*

THE DINOSAUR AGE
The first land-
dwelling dinosaurs
appeared during the
Triassic, Jurassic,
and Cretaceous
periods. This skeleton is from
Dilophosaurus, an agile, predatory
dinosaur from the Jurassic period.

HOMO
HABILIS
SKULL

EARLY HUMANS
Homo habilis (handy man) is an
early human, dating from the
Quaternary period. The name of
this ancestor comes from the fossil
evidence that the early human was
skilled in using sophisticated tools.

GEOLOGICAL TIMESCALE		
ERA	PERIOD: MILLIONS OF YEARS AGO (MYA)	
CENOZOIC	QUATERNARY 2 MYA–PRESENT	
	TERTIARY 65–2 MYA	
MESOZOIC	CRETACEOUS 146–65 MYA	
	JURASSIC 208–146 MYA	
	TRIASSIC 245–208 MYA	
PALEOZOIC	PERMIAN 290–245 MYA	
	CARBONIFEROUS 363–290 MYA	
	DEVONIAN 409–363 MYA	
	SILURIAN 439–409 MYA	
	ORDOVICIAN 510–439 MYA	
	CAMBRIAN 570–510 MYA	
	PRECAMBRIAN 4,600–570 MYA	

SLATE MOUNTAINS
Fine-grained slate forms from sedimentary rocks. Rocks such as shale or mudstone are compressed during mountain building and changed into slate. Slate's aligned crystals mean that it splits, or cleaves, easily into flat sheets.

METAMORPHIC ROCKS

SEDIMENTARY, metamorphic, or igneous rocks are remade into new metamorphic rocks. The rock doesn't melt but it is changed underground by pressure and heat. During mountain building, in particular, intense pressure over millions of years alters the texture and nature of rocks. Igneous rocks such as granite change into gneiss and sedimentary rocks like limestone into marble.

Carved white marble

MARBLE SCULPTURE
Michelangelo's statue of David is carved in marble. Marble comes in many varieties and is often used in buildings. It is also easy to cut.

METAMORPHIC FACTS

• The oldest rock on Earth is a metamorphic rock. It is Amitsoc gneiss from Amitsoc Bay, Greenland.

• Rubies are found in metamorphic limestone in the Himalayas. They formed during mountain building.

REGIONAL METAMORPHISM

Extreme pressure and heat as a result of mountain building lead to regional metamorphism. Metamorphism on this scale can cover a vast area.

Intrusive igneous rock exposed by weathering

Aureole (area where metamorphism has taken place)

Migmatite showing swirls of folded rock

CONTACT METAMORPHISM

Rocks near to a lava flow or to an intrusion of igneous rock can be altered by contact metamorphism. This metamorphism affects a small area and is generated by heat alone.

TYPES OF METAMORPHIC ROCK

SLATE

Mica crystals lie in the same direction in slate, making it easy to split.

MARBLE

When limestone is subjected to intense heat it becomes marble.

SCHIST

Formed in moderate pressure and temperature conditions, schist often shows small, wavy folds.

GNEISS

Igneous and sedimentary rocks can become gneiss. It forms at high temperatures.

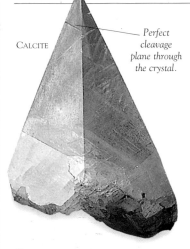

CALCITE

Perfect cleavage plane through the crystal.

MINERALS

ROCKS ARE MADE from non-living, natural substances called minerals, which may be alone or in combination. Marble is pure calcite, for example, but granite is a mixture of quartz, feldspars, and mica. Most minerals are formed from silicates (compounds of oxygen and silicon). Minerals with a regular arrangement of atoms may form crystals. To identify a mineral, properties such as crystal structure, colour, and hardness are tested.

CLEAVAGE AND FRACTURE
Diamond and calcite cleave when they break. Cleavage is a smooth break between layers of atoms in a crystal. A fracture is an uneven break, not related to the internal atomic structure. Most minerals fracture and cleave.

MOHS' SCALE	1	2	3	4
A German mineralogist named Friedrich Mohs devised a scale to compare the hardness of different minerals. A mineral is able to scratch any others below it on the scale and can be scratched by any mineral above it.	TALC	GYPSUM	CALCITE	FLUORITE

MINERAL FACTS

- Only a diamond will scratch a diamond.
- Quartz is found in igneous, sedimentary, and metamorphic rock.
- The word "crystal" comes from a Greek word *kyros* meaning "icy cold".

PLAGIOCLASE FELDSPAR

FELDSPAR
This abundant rock-forming mineral is in both basalt and granite.

QUARTZ OR ROCK CRYSTAL

QUARTZ
A common mineral, quartz comes in many different colours. Amethyst and citrine are varieties of quartz.

COLOUR STREAKS
Scratching a mineral on an unglazed tile produces a coloured streak. The colour of the powder left behind is known as the mineral's streak.

ORPIMENT – GOLDEN

HEMATITE – RED/BROWN

A light aluminium-rich mica

MUSCOVITE

MICA
Found in metamorphic rocks such as schists and slate, flaky mica is also in igneous rocks like granite.

5	6	7	8	9	10
APATITE	ORTHOCLASE FELDSPAR	QUARTZ	TOPAZ	CORUNDUM	DIAMOND

GEMSTONES

ONLY ABOUT 50 OF Earth's 3,000 minerals are valued as gemstones. Minerals such as diamonds, sapphires, emeralds, and rubies are commonly used as gems. They are chosen for their rarity, durability, colour, and optical qualities. Gems may be found embedded in rocks or washed into the gravel of a river. Organic gemstones have a plant or animal origin. They include pearl, amber, and coral.

Red spinels were often mistaken for rubies

The crown contains more than 3,000 stones

CROWN JEWELS
The British Imperial State Crown contains the Black Prince's ruby (in fact a 170-carat spinel) and the famous Cullinan II diamond.

EMERALD
Green beryl crystals called emeralds contain chromium to make them green. Most emeralds are mined in Colombia. They rate 7.5 on Mohs' scale of hardness.

Emerald is found in granites and pegmatites

KIMBERLITE
Diamonds used to be found mainly in river gravels in India. In 1870 diamonds were discovered in volcanic rock, called kimberlite, in South Africa.

BRILLIANT
Skilled gem cutters, known as lapidaries, cut a rough crystal into a sparkling stone. A diamond has 57 facets or faces ground onto it to make it a brilliant.

SYNTHETIC GEMS

Some gems can be reproduced almost exactly in a laboratory. Dissolved minerals and colouring agents crystallize under strictly controlled conditions to produce perfect crystals. Synthetic crystals are used in medicine and the electronics industry.

NATURAL RUBY

SYNTHETIC RUBY

GEMSTONE FACTS

• The Cullinan is the largest diamond ever found. It weighed 3,106 carats (0.6 kg/1.37 lb).

• About one in every 1,000 oysters contains a pearl, and about one in every 3,000 mussels.

• A carat equals 0.2 g (0.007 oz).

IMITATION TURQUOISE

REAL TURQUOISE

IMITATION GEMS

Glass or plastic may be used to imitate gems. The optical properties of such imitations are different from those of the genuine gem.

PEARL

Shellfish, such as mussels and oysters, grow pearls in their shells. When a grain of sand lodges in its shell, the animal covers it with nacre, a substance to stop irritation. This creates a pearl.

AMBER

Fossilized tree resin from coniferous trees is called amber. The trees that yielded this amber existed more than 300 million years ago and are extinct. Amber may contain insects trapped in the tree sap.

MINERAL RESOURCES

ORE MINERALS

A ROCK THAT yields metal in sufficient amounts is a metallic ore. Gold and copper can be found as pure metals, that is, uncombined with any other elements. Most other metals, such as iron and tin, are extracted from ores. After mining or quarrying, the ores are crushed, and the metal separated and then purified.

IRON ORE
(HEMATITE)

ALUMINIUM ORE
(BAUXITE)

ALUMINIUM
KITCHEN FOIL

ALUMINIUM
Lightweight aluminium is a good conductor of electricity and resists corrosion. It is extracted from its main ore (bauxite) by passing an electric current through a rock solution. It is used for power lines.

GOLD FACTS

• The largest pure gold nugget weighed 70.9 kg (156.3 lb). It was found in Victoria, Australia.

• 60 per cent of the world's gold is mined in South Africa.

• Gold never loses its lustre or shine.

• It is said that all the gold ever mined would fit into an average four-bedroomed house.

IRON
Hematite is an important iron ore. Iron can be cast, forged, and alloyed with other metals. Steel, used in ship-building and industry, is produced using iron.

MERCURY
THERMOMETER

MERCURY ORE
(CINNABAR)

MERCURY
The primary mercury ore is called cinnabar. It is found near volcanic vents and hot springs, mostly in China, Spain, and Italy. Mercury is liquid at room temperature.

MINING
Blasting and boring rock in underground mines allows recovery of ores such as gold or tin. Dredging gravel or quarrying rock also retrieves ores.

GRAINS
OF GOLD

VEINS OF
GOLD
IN QUARTZ

GOLD
Veins of gold occur in quartz. Panning or larger-scale dredging can retrieve gold grains from sand or river gravel deposits. About 1,500 tonnes (tons) of gold are produced each year.

GOLD GRIFFIN
BRACELET

FOSSIL FUELS: COAL

PEAT

LIGNITE

BITUMINOUS COAL

ANTHRACITE

PLANTS THAT GREW millions of years ago slowly changed to form coal. Vegetation in swamp areas, buried under layers of sediment, forms a substance called peat. Peat, in turn, is pressed into a soft coal called lignite. Soft bituminous coal forms under further pressure. Anthracite is the hardest and most compressed coal. When coal burns, the energy of the ancient plants is released. Coal is used to fuel power stations that produce electricity. Coal supplies, like oil, are finite.

FROM PEAT TO COAL
Heat and pressure change crumbly brown peat into shiny black anthracite coal.

COAL FORMATION

Vegetation

Layers of sediment

Temperature and pressure increases

PEAT LAYER
In swamps, when plants decay they form a compact layer called peat. This material is 60 per cent carbon and can be burnt as a fuel.

COAL LAYER
Buried beneath sediment layers compacted peat forms coal. Lignite is the softest coal and anthracite the hardest coal.

INSIDE A COAL MINE
To reach a seam, or layer, of coal underground, rock must be blasted and bored away. Shafts go down from the surface to tunnels at different levels. Rock pillars and walls support the roof.

Buildings on the surface

Air shaft

Lift cage for miners

Train to carry miners to the cutting face

Coal is hauled to the surface

Cutting head

COAL MINING
People have mined coal since about 500 B.C. Today's miners use drills and computer-controlled machines. Special cutting machines dig out the coal at the coal face. Deep coal mines deliver 2,000 tonnes (tons) of coal a day.

MAP OF COAL DEPOSITS
Swampy forests covered parts of Europe, Asia, and North America, which were low-lying during the Carboniferous period (360–286 million years ago). These tropical forest areas provide most of the coal deposits that are mined today.

The Russian Federation has 23 per cent of all known coal reserves

FOSSIL FUELS: OIL AND GAS

MOST SCIENTISTS believe oil and gas are the remains of marine animals. The organisms were broken down over millions of years and compressed to form oil and gas (they are usually found together). The modern world relies heavily on these fuels, especially oil refined into petrol. However, when oil burns it causes pollution.

OIL RIG
An oil production platform floats but is tethered to the seabed. Oil is pumped up long pipelines to the oil platform.

OIL AND GAS FORMATION

Tiny marine organisms

New layers of sediment

Oil and gas rigs

Fuels collect under solid caprock

STAGE 1
Decaying plants and animals sink to the sea floor. They lie trapped under sediment layers.

STAGE 2
Heat increases as the sediments sink deeper. The organic remains become oil and gas.

STAGE 3
Oil and gas molecules rise through permeable rock. The fuels collect in porous rock.

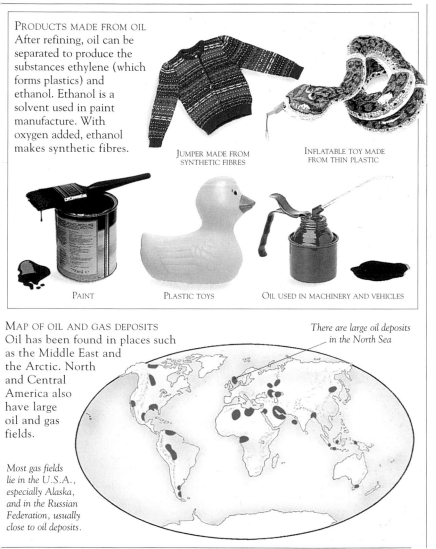

PRODUCTS MADE FROM OIL
After refining, oil can be separated to produce the substances ethylene (which forms plastics) and ethanol. Ethanol is a solvent used in paint manufacture. With oxygen added, ethanol makes synthetic fibres.

JUMPER MADE FROM SYNTHETIC FIBRES

INFLATABLE TOY MADE FROM THIN PLASTIC

PAINT

PLASTIC TOYS

OIL USED IN MACHINERY AND VEHICLES

MAP OF OIL AND GAS DEPOSITS
Oil has been found in places such as the Middle East and the Arctic. North and Central America also have large oil and gas fields.

There are large oil deposits in the North Sea

Most gas fields lie in the U.S.A., especially Alaska, and in the Russian Federation, usually close to oil deposits.

OTHER SOURCES OF ENERGY

MOST OF THE energy the world uses
for cooking, heating, or industry is
produced by burning fossil fuels. As
well as causing pollution, these fuels
will eventually run out. The Sun,
wind, or water can be used to create
pollution-free energy. This energy
is renewable for as long as the Sun
shines, the wind blows, and the tides
rise and fall. Much of the energy
we use in our homes is generated
at nuclear power stations.

SOLAR ENERGY
The Sun's light energy is
captured by huge mirrors.
The energy is used to
generate electricity.

TIDAL POWER
Water is held on one side of this
power station which is built across an
estuary. At high tide water accumulates,
then it is allowed to flow through the
barrage, or dam. The force of the
water-flow drives several turbines.

A barrage holds
back the water
at high tide

Barrage acts
as a road
bridge

Barriers control the
flow of water from one
side to the other

The turbine drives
electricity generators

Direction of water flow

Water held behind a dam

Energy is transferred from the turbine to the generator

Water flow turns the turbine

WATER POWER

A hydroelectric power station uses water power to produce electricity. The energy created by falling water drives a turbine. A turbine is then used to power an electric generator.

NUCLEAR ENERGY

Elements such as plutonium and uranium are used in nuclear power stations to generate energy. An atom of uranium can be split using a particle called a neutron. This produces heat and other neutrons. In turn, these neutrons split more atoms, generating further energy.

Neutron hits uranium atom

The nucleus of the uranium atom splits

More neutrons are made

ENERGY FACTS

• The first tidal power station opened in La Rance, France in 1966.

• Nuclear power first produced electricity in the U.S.A. in 1951.

• Hydroelectric power stations generate five per cent of all electricity.

WIND POWER

California, U.S.A. has wind farms that contain thousands of windmills. Wind spins the propellers, which drive electric generators. Each windmill can produce up to four megawatts of power.

OTHER SOURCES OF ENERGY

MOUNTAINS, VALLEYS, AND CAVES

THE WORLD'S MOUNTAINS

THE HIGHEST POINTS on Earth result from a collision of Earth's tectonic plates. The highest range of mountains is the Himalayas in Asia. These lofty peaks continue to grow as the Indian plate pushes the Eurasian plate. As the rocky plates fracture and crumple (or fault and fold) a mountain range takes shape. Our planet has had several mountain-building episodes during its history. Some mountains continue to rise though all are being weathered away.

ANCIENT MOUNTAINS
The Scottish Highlands have been eroded into soft rounded hills. The ancient mountains formed more than 250 million years ago.

YOUNG MOUNTAINS
Mountains such as the Himalayas continue to rise. The mountains are about 50 million years old and have jagged peaks.

TYPES OF MOUNTAIN

FAULT-BLOCK MOUNTAIN
When Earth's plates push into one another, faults or cracks in the crust appear. Huge blocks of rock are forced upwards.

FOLD MOUNTAIN
At the meeting of two of Earth's plates, the crust buckles and bends. The rocky crust is forced up into a mountain range.

MOUNTAINS AND MOUNTAIN RANGES

The world's longest mountain ranges usually follow the edges of the Earth's plates. Where plates collide they crumple and fold.

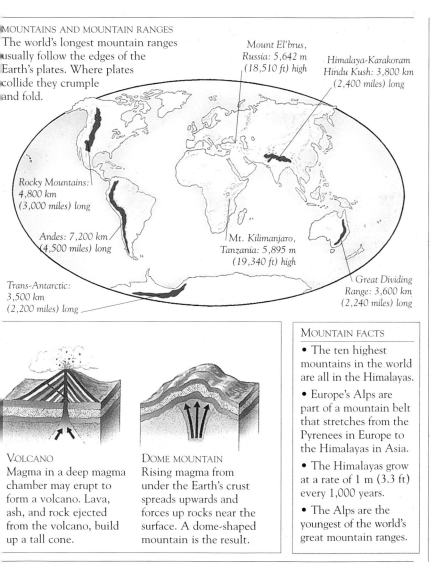

Mount El'brus, Russia: 5,642 m (18,510 ft) high

Himalaya-Karakoram Hindu Kush: 3,800 km (2,400 miles) long

Rocky Mountains: 4,800 km (3,000 miles) long

Andes: 7,200 km (4,500 miles) long

Mt. Kilimanjaro, Tanzania: 5,895 m (19,340 ft) high

Trans-Antarctic: 3,500 km (2,200 miles) long

Great Dividing Range: 3,600 km (2,240 miles) long

VOLCANO
Magma in a deep magma chamber may erupt to form a volcano. Lava, ash, and rock ejected from the volcano, build up a tall cone.

DOME MOUNTAIN
Rising magma from under the Earth's crust spreads upwards and forces up rocks near the surface. A dome-shaped mountain is the result.

MOUNTAIN FACTS
• The ten highest mountains in the world are all in the Himalayas.

• Europe's Alps are part of a mountain belt that stretches from the Pyrenees in Europe to the Himalayas in Asia.

• The Himalayas grow at a rate of 1 m (3.3 ft) every 1,000 years.

• The Alps are the youngest of the world's great mountain ranges.

MOUNTAIN FEATURES

CONDITIONS ON MOUNTAINS can be harsh. As altitude increases temperature drops, air becomes thinner, and winds blow harder. Animal and plant life has adapted to survive in this environment. Mountains can be divided into several separate zones. The zones are similar whether the mountain lies in a tropical or temperate area and whether it is an isolated volcanic peak or part of a mountain range.

MOUNT KILIMANJARO
Africa's tallest mountain is Mount Kilimanjaro in Tanzania. It is a solitary peak, not part of a range. In fact, it is a dormant volcanic cone. Despite lying near the equator, Kilimanjaro is permanently snow-capped.

WORLD'S HIGHEST MOUNTAINS			
MOUNTAIN	LOCATION	HEIGHT IN METRES	HEIGHT IN FEET
Mt. Everest, Nepal	Asia	8,848	29,028
Mt. Aconcagua, Argentina	South America	6,960	22,834
Mt. McKinley, Alaska	North America	6,194	20,320
Mt. Kilimanjaro, Tanzania	Africa	5,895	19,340
Mt. El'brus, Russia	Europe	5,642	18,510
Vinson Massif	Antarctica	5,140	16,863
Mt. Wilhelm, Papua New Guinea	Australasia	4,884	16,024

THE ANDES
The world's longest range of mountains is the Andes in South America. The chain stretches for 7,200 km (4,500 miles).

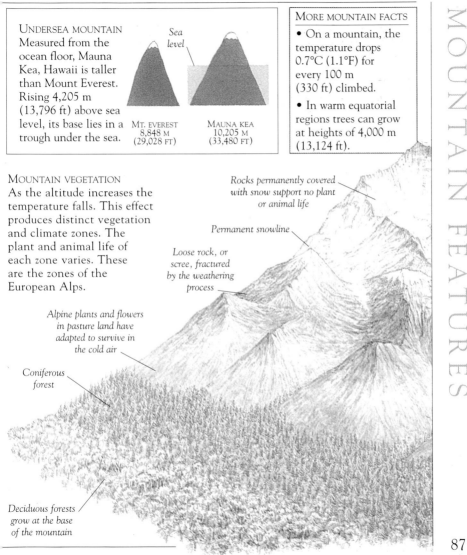

UNDERSEA MOUNTAIN
Measured from the ocean floor, Mauna Kea, Hawaii is taller than Mount Everest. Rising 4,205 m (13,796 ft) above sea level, its base lies in a trough under the sea.

Sea level

MT. EVEREST
8,848 M
(29,028 FT)

MAUNA KEA
10,205 M
(33,480 FT)

MORE MOUNTAIN FACTS
• On a mountain, the temperature drops 0.7°C (1.1°F) for every 100 m (330 ft) climbed.

• In warm equatorial regions trees can grow at heights of 4,000 m (13,124 ft).

MOUNTAIN VEGETATION
As the altitude increases the temperature falls. This effect produces distinct vegetation and climate zones. The plant and animal life of each zone varies. These are the zones of the European Alps.

Rocks permanently covered with snow support no plant or animal life

Permanent snowline

Loose rock, or scree, fractured by the weathering process

Alpine plants and flowers in pasture land have adapted to survive in the cold air

Coniferous forest

Deciduous forests grow at the base of the mountain

GORGE
A ravine with steep sides is called a gorge. A canyon is similar to a gorge but it is usually found in desert areas.

VALLEYS

FORCES OF EROSION, especially water, carve out the shape of the landscape. Steep-sided valleys can be cut out by fast-flowing mountain streams. Larger rivers wear a path through the land, shaping wide, flat valleys as they near the sea. Frozen water in glaciers also erodes rock, forming deep, icy gullies. Valleys sometimes form as a result of crustal movements that pull rocks apart at a fault in the Earth's surface.

Land drops between the plate edges

RIFT VALLEY
Faults occur in the Earth's crust where two plates are moving apart. A long, straight valley, such as the African Rift Valley, forms between the faults.

Rivers shed their sediments on the flat flood plain

A fan-shaped delta forms at the river

FJORD
Steep-sided inlets in Norway and New Zealand are caused by glaciers deepening river valleys. As the ice melts and the sea level rises these fjords become flooded.

VALLEY FACTS
• Africa's Rift Valley stretches for 4,000 km (2,500 miles).
• The longest fjord, in Nordvest, Greenland, is 313 km (194 miles) long.

RIVER VALLEY FEATURES
In the mountains, a fast-flowing stream cuts through rock creating a steep gully. In the middle part of the river, the water meanders across a broad valley. Near the sea, the river flows across a flat plain or it may fan out into a delta.

Rainfall runs down gullies

V-shape of a river valley's upper course

The river curves back and forth in a series of meanders

Oxbow lake forms where a meander is cut off

The river valley becomes wider and flatter and the water flows more slowly

Broad shape of valley at river mouth

WADI
In deserts it rains rarely, often less than 250 mm (10 in) a year. A torrential downpour in such an arid area can cause a flash flood. The rain carves out a channel called a wadi. Water runs down these dry river valleys carrying rocks and debris with it.

CAVES

UNDERGROUND CAVERNS and caves occur in several types of landscape. Different processes are responsible for the different sorts of cave. The action of ice, lava, waves, and rainwater cause subterranean openings. In particular, rainwater has a spectacular effect on limestone, producing vast caverns full of unusual shapes.

ICE CAVE
Beneath a glacier there is sometimes a stream of water that has thawed, called meltwater. The water can wear away an ice cave full of icicles in the glacier.

INSIDE A LIMESTONE CAVE
Carbonic acid in rain seeps into cracks in limestone and dissolves the rock. Underground tunnels and caves form as water eats away the rock. Streams may flow down sink holes in the rock into a cave system and emerge in another place.

A stream may disappear down a sink hole.

Stalactites hang down from the roof.

Columns form where stalactites and stalagmites join.

Water seeps into cracks in rocks.

Stalagmites grow upwards from the cave floor.

LAVA CAVE
Some lava cools to form a thick crust. Below the crust a tube of molten lava flows. When it empties a cave is left.

SEA CAVE
Caves may form at the base of cliffs undercut by waves. A cave can be worn through to form an arch. The top of this arch may eventually collapse and leave an isolated stack to be buffeted by the waves.

CAVE FACTS
• Jean Bernard cave in France is the deepest in the world. It is 1,602 m (5,256 ft) deep.

• The longest stalactite – 6.2 m (20.4 ft) long – is in Co. Clare, Ireland.

• The tallest stalagmite is 32 m (105 ft) high. It is in the Czech Republic.

• America's Mammoth Cave system, Kentucky, is the world's longest cave system. It is 560 km (348 miles) long.

STALAGMITES AND STALACTITES

STALACTITE
In limestone caves, deposits of calcite in dripping water create distinctive features, such as stalactites. These grow from the ceiling of the cave towards the floor.

COLUMNS
Mineral deposits construct stalactites and stalagmites in caves. If the two shapes meet, they form a column.

STALAGMITE
It may take several thousand years for a stalagmite to grow 2.5 cm (1 in) – drip by drip from a cave floor to the roof.

GLACIATION

THE WORLD'S GLACIERS

A GLACIER IS a moving ice mass that results from more snow falling in winter than melts in the summer. In mountain regions glaciers form when snow builds up, pressing down on older snow and squeezing out the air. The compressed ice will eventually begin to move downhill. This frozen "river" carries a great deal of debris. Surrounding rock is scoured by the ice and sediment as it travels down the valley. In this way glaciers leave their mark on the landscape.

GLACIAL DEBRIS
Rocks are smoothed when they are plucked up and carried along by a glacier. This rock has scratches, or striae, too.

Ridge or arête between two glaciers

Medial moraine – debris carried in the middle of the glacier

When the ice moves over a sharp incline, it cracks to form crevasses

THE WORLD'S LONGEST GLACIERS		
GLACIERS	LENGTH IN KM	LENGTH IN MILES
Lambert-Fisher Ice Passage, Antarctica	515	320
Novaya Zemlya, Russia	418	260
Arctic Institute Ice Passage, Antarctica	362	225
Nimrod-Lennox-King, Antarctica	289	180
Denman Glacier, Antarctica	241	150
Beardmore Glacier, Antarctica	225	140
Recovery Glacier, Antarctica	200	124

BEFORE GLACIATION

The mountain valley carved out by a river is usually steep and shaped like a letter V.

AFTER GLACIATION

A mountain glacier flows along the path of a river. The V-shape is eroded by the glacier into a U-shape.

CROSS-SECTION OF A GLACIER

Cirque or corrie – hollow where glacier begins

Compact snow called firn

FEATURES OF A GLACIER

A glacier begins high in the mountains in hollows called cirques. New snow builds up and becomes compacted, forming denser ice called firn. As the glacier moves downhill it collects rock from the floor and sides of the valley and carries it along. Eventually the glacier reaches a point where it melts and drops its load of rocky debris, or moraine.

The snout or front of the glacier

Meltwater flows from the snout

Pile of rocks and boulders called terminal moraine

ICE CAPS AND ICE AGES

ANTARCTICA AND GREENLAND are blanketed in ice sheets up to 3,500 m (11,500 ft) thick. Many winters of snowfall accumulate to produce an ice cap, which eventually moves downhill as a broad glacier. In Earth's history, periods of extreme cold, called ice ages, brought glacial conditions as far south as Europe and North America. Our mild climate may only be an interval between ice ages.

ICE CAP
Vast ice sheets covering Antarctica and Greenland are known as ice caps. This type of glacier originates in cold regions of the world; other glaciers are in mountainous areas.

FORMATION OF AN ICE CAP
Layers of snow build up during the winter months and become icy firn. Over several years, the result is a thick ice cap. Gravity pulls the ice down to the edges of the land.

Accumulation of compacted snow called firn

Isolated peaks, called nunataks, are free from ice.

Glaciers form as ice moves downhill

Direction of wind

Ice shelf, where ice floats out to sea

Flat-topped or tabular iceberg

GRAPH OF THE EARTH'S TEMPERATURE

The low points on the graph show the last five occasions when the average temperature on Earth was cold enough to allow major glacial advances.

CLIMATE	
°C	°F
17	63
16	61
15	59
14	57
13	56
12	54

YEARS AGO   600,000   400,000   200,000   PRESENT DAY

ICE FACTS

• Most of the world's fresh water – 75 per cent of it – is stored in ice caps and glaciers.

• About 12 per cent of the sea and 10 per cent of the land on Earth is covered in ice.

• Almost 90 per cent of the world's ice lies in the continent of Antarctica.

ICE AGES

During the last ice age, about 30,000 years ago, ice sheets covered a large part of the planet, particularly North America and Europe. All ice ages are interspersed with warmer periods called interglacials. Ice advanced and retreated with each major temperature change.

PLEISTOCENE EPOCH – THE LAST ICE AGE

EXTENT OF ICE IN THE WORLD TODAY

SCIENTISTS EXAMINE A BABY MAMMOTH FOUND IN THE ICE

WOOLLY MAMMOTH

In Siberia, the remains of extinct animals called mammoths have been found in ice. They froze so quickly that their bodies were preserved virtually intact. These elephant-like mammals had curled tusks and woolly coats and lived during the last ice age.

97

AVALANCHES AND ICEBERGS

MOUNTAINS ARE inhospitable places. Winter snowstorms pile up layers of ice and snow. The layers may become unstable and rush down the mountain in an avalanche, sweeping away anything in their path. Ships at sea must contend with another icy hazard: icebergs, formed when large chunks of ice break off coastal glaciers or ice shelves and float out to sea.

SEA ICE
Seawater freezes when it reaches –1.9°C (28°F). Sea ice is never more than about 5 m (16 ft) thick. It can be used as a source of fresh water because the salt is left behind in the sea.

AVALANCHE
Vibrations, from noise and minor earthquakes, combined with a rise in temperature, especially in spring, can trigger a fall of snow, called an avalanche.

A heavy snowfall adds weight to the snow cover

More snow joins the avalanche as it tumbles down the mountain

SNOWLINE

There is an imaginary line on a mountainside, called the snowline, below which snow melts during summer. Above this line the snow remains throughout the year. The snowline is higher in areas nearer the equator.

The snowline in the European Alps is at about 2,700 m (9,000 ft) high

In Antarctica, the snowline is at or near sea level

On the equator the snowline is 4,900 m (16,000 ft) high

ICEBERGS

Glaciers and the floating edges of ice caps lose chunks of ice called icebergs into the sea, a process known as calving. All icebergs are frozen fresh water, rather than frozen sea water.

ICEBERG FACTS

- Only 12 per cent of an iceberg can be seen above the ocean; 88 per cent is under the water.

- The tallest iceberg was sighted in 1958 off Greenland. It was 167 m (550 ft) high.

- The largest iceberg, spotted in the Pacific Ocean in 1956, had an area of 32,500 km^2 (12,500 miles^2).

OCEANS, ISLANDS, AND COASTS

THE WORLD'S OCEANS

SEEN FROM SPACE, the Earth looks blue and watery. This is because two-thirds of it is covered with water. The water is held in oceans and seas. (Seas are surrounded by land.) Three of the five oceans are in the southern hemisphere. Major currents circulate the oceans anti-clockwise in the southern hemisphere and clockwise in the northern hemisphere.

THE WORLD'S LARGEST OCEANS AND SEAS		
OCEAN OR SEA	AREA IN KM²	AREA IN MILES²
Pacific Ocean	166,229,000	64,181,000
Atlantic Ocean	86,551,000	33,417,000
Indian Ocean	73,422,000	28,348,000
Arctic Ocean	13,223,000	5,105,000
South China Sea	2,975,000	1,149,000
Caribbean Sea	2,516,000	917,000
Mediterranean Sea	2,509,000	969,000
Bering Sea	2,261,000	873,000

FORMATION OF OCEANS

THE ATMOSPHERE FORMS
The semi-molten surface of the Earth was covered by volcanoes. Hot gases and water vapour emitted by volcanoes formed the Earth's early atmosphere.

THE RAINS FALL
The water vapour in this early atmosphere condensed as rain. Rainstorms poured down on the planet and filled the vast hollows on the Earth's surface.

THE OCEANS FORM
These huge pools became the oceans. The water was hot and acidic. Later, plant life evolved and produced oxygen for the atmosphere and oceans.

OCEAN ZONES
Oceanographers split
the oceans into zones
according to depth.
Only water near the
surface is sunlit. At
greater depths the
water is colder and
darker. Pressure also
increases with depth.
Sea creatures have
adapted to conditions
in the different zones.

*The temperature
deep in the ocean is
nearly freezing*

*Bathal zone:
to 2,000 m (6,560 ft)*

*Light seldom
penetrates more than
100 m (330 ft).*

*Abyssal zone:
2,000–6,000 m
(6,560–
19,690 ft)*

*Hadal zone:
below 6,000 m
(19,690 ft)*

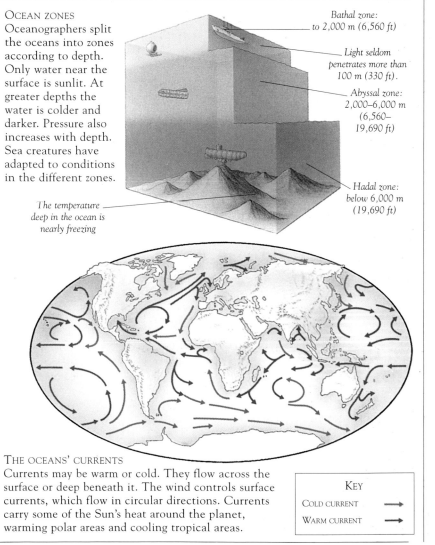

THE OCEANS' CURRENTS
Currents may be warm or cold. They flow across the
surface or deep beneath it. The wind controls surface
currents, which flow in circular directions. Currents
carry some of the Sun's heat around the planet,
warming polar areas and cooling tropical areas.

KEY	
COLD CURRENT	→
WARM CURRENT	→

WAVES AND TIDES

THE OCEANS AND seas are always moving. Buffeted by the wind and heated by the Sun, waves and currents form in the oceans. Ripples on the surface of the water grow into waves that pound the shore and shape coastlines. The Moon's and Sun's gravity pull the oceans, causing a daily and monthly cycle of tides.

WHIRLPOOL
An uneven seafloor can cause several tidal flows to collide. The currents surge upwards and rush into each other. Eddies and whirlpools form at the surface.

Rotation of the Earth balances the Moon's gravitational pull.

MONTHLY TIDES
High and low tides occur daily or twice daily. Twice each month, tides are greater (spring tides) or smaller (neap tides). This cycle of tides depends on the relative positions of the Moon, Sun, and Earth.

SPRING TIDES
The Sun, Earth, and Moon are aligned to create spring tides.

The Moon's gravity pulls the oceans.

The oceans on each side of the Earth rise approximately every 12 hours and then fall back.

NEAP TIDES
Opposing pulls of Sun and Moon cause neap tides.

Earth's spinning on its axis affects the tides.

GULF STREAM

A current of warm water called the Gulf Stream moves from the Gulf of Mexico across the Atlantic, bringing mild winter weather to the western coasts of Europe. Like a huge river at sea, the Gulf Stream flows 160 km (100 miles) a day. This current or gyre is 60 km (37 miles) wide and 600 m (2,000 ft) deep. As the Gulf Stream nears Europe it is called the North Atlantic Drift.

EUROPE

NORTH AMERICA

Gulf Stream

GULF OF MEXICO

The warm water slows and spreads out as it nears Europe

The top part of the wave, the crest, continues up the beach

Particles near the surface turn over and over

The beach slows down the base of the wave

WAVE MOVEMENT

The wind blows waves towards the shore. But it is not the water particles that travel, only the wave form. The particles rotate as each wave passes and return to their original position.

WAVE FACTS

• The highest recorded wave was seen in the western Pacific. It was 34 m (112 ft) high from trough to crest.

• The Antarctic Circumpolar Current flows at a rate of 130 million m³ (4,600 million ft³) per second.

• Hawaiian tides rise 45 cm (12 in) a day.

COMPOSITION OF SEAWATER

The oceans contain dissolved minerals, some washed from the land by rivers. The predominant constituents of seawater are sodium and chloride which together form salt. The oceans are about 35 parts water to one part salt.

Other chemicals 1.9%
Potassium 1.1%
Calcium 1.2%
Magnesium 3.7%
Sulphate 7.6%
Sodium 30.2%
Chloride 54.3%

THE OCEAN FLOOR

THE WORLD UNDER the oceans has both strange and familiar features. Similar to a landscape on dry ground, mountains, valleys, and volcanoes dot the ocean floor. Once scientists had equipment to explore the ocean bed, they discovered that tectonic plate movement had caused many ocean floor features, including trenches, seamounts, and submarine canyons.

MAPPING THE OCEAN
Oceanographers use echo-sounding, which bounces signals off the ocean bed, to map the ocean floor's contours.

FEATURES OF THE OCEAN FLOOR

Island arc

Guyot is a flat-topped seamount

Spreading ridge

Deep sea trench

One plate is subducted under another

TRENCH
Where the ocean floor sinks into the mantle, long, deep trenches occur.

ISLAND ARC
When oceanic plates collide, one plate is subducted and melts. Magma rises through the upper plate to form an arc of volcanic islands.

DEEP-SEA EXPLORATION

DIVERS AND VEHICLES	DEPTH IN METRES	DEPTH IN FEET
Sponge diver holding breath	15	49
Air/SCUBA sports diver	50	164
Oil rig divers with diving bell	250	820
Deepest experimental dive	500	1,640
Barton's benthoscope	1,370	4,494
Cousteau diving saucer	3,350	11,000
Shinkai submersible	6,500	21,325
Trieste bathyscape	10,911	35,800

BATHYSCAPE
The deepest dive was made by the bathyscape *Trieste* in 1960. It dived in the world's deepest trench, the Mariana Trench.

SEAMOUNT
An underwater volcano that rises over 1,000 m (3,280 ft) is a seamount.

ABYSSAL PLAIN
This sediment-covered plain lies at a depth of about 4,000 m (15,000 ft).

SUBMARINE CANYON
Rivers of sediment flowing from the continental shelf can erode deep canyons.

Two of the Earth's tectonic plates are moving apart

Seamount

Submarine canyon

Continental shelf

Abyssal plain

Continental slope

Magma rises between the plates

Continental rise

MID-OCEANIC RIDGE
Magma rising between two tectonic plates forms a ridge.

CONTINENTAL SLOPE
The continental slope descends steeply from the continental shelf towards the abyssal plain, flattening out along the gently sloping continental rise.

CONTINENTAL SHELF
Stretching from the edge of the land like a vast ledge under the sea, the continental shelf can be 70 km (43 miles) wide. The ocean here is about 250 m (1,600 ft) deep.

OCEAN FEATURES

OCEANS ARE a rich source of many useful substances. Seawater contains nutrients and minerals. Deposits of oil and gas are found in continental shelf sediment. Metals such as gold and manganese are present in sediments on the ocean floor. Near ocean ridges, the sea may contain minerals from inside the Earth.

BLACK SMOKERS
In 1977, scientists discovered strange chimneys, formed from minerals on the ocean floor, called black smokers. In rift valleys between spreading ridges, they eject water as hot as 300°C (572°F) and minerals such as sulphur.

The vent minerals colour the water black

Jets of hot water shoot from the chimneys

Smokers can grow as tall as 10 m (33 ft)

Tube worms and giant clams live on bacteria near the vents

THE WORLD'S DEEPEST SEA TRENCHES		
TRENCH	DEPTH IN METRES	DEPTH IN FEET
Mariana Trench, West Pacific	10,920	35,827
Tonga Trench, South Pacific	10,800	35,433
Philippine Trench, West Pacific	10,057	32,995
Kermadec Trench, South Pacific	10,047	32,961
Izu-Ogasawara Trench, West Pacific	9,780	32,087

OCEAN PRODUCT FACTS
• There are 0.000004 parts per million of gold in the ocean.

• It takes a million years for a manganese nodule to grow 2 mm (0.08 in) in diameter.

OCEAN PRODUCTS

MANGANESE
Nodules from the seabed are used in industry.

OIL
This is a non-renewable fossil fuel. It is pumped from rocks in the continental shelf.

SAND
Rock pounded by waves becomes sand. In volcanic areas it is black.

LIMESTONE
Like sand, limestone is found mostly in coastal waters.

Diamonds in gravel are known as alluvial diamonds.

DIAMONDS IN GRAVEL
In shallow waters off the coasts of Africa and Indonesia, diamonds can be found in continental shelf gravels. Most have been washed down by rivers into the sea.

OCEAN FLOOR SEDIMENT
The continental shelf is covered with sand, mud, and silt washed onto it from rivers. In the deep ocean, the floor is coated with ooze. This contains remains of dead marine life.

Rock is carried 500 km (311 miles) from the ridge over 5 million years. Sediment gathers

After 10 million years the rock has moved farther from the ridge. It is now covered with thick sediment

New rock erupted from the mantle at mid-ocean ridges has no sediment cover

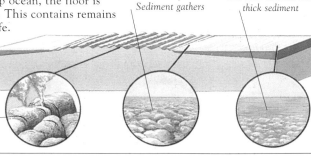

109

ISLANDS

A PIECE OF LAND smaller than a continent and surrounded by water is called an island. Magma rising from volcanic vents in the crust creates islands in the sea. An arc of islands appears where a tectonic plate is subducted. Some islands exist only when the tide is high; at low tide it is possible to walk to these islands. Small islands may exist in rivers and lakes. In warmer regions coral reefs may grow from the sea, built by living organisms.

Causeway

A narrow strip of land links the island to the shore.

CAUSEWAY
A change in sea level can create an island. Land may be accessible only at low tide by a causeway. At high tide the island is cut off.

ISLAND FACTS

• Bouvet Island is the most remote island – 1,700 km (1,056 miles) from the nearest landmass (Antarctica).

• Kwejalein in the Marshall Islands, in the Pacific Ocean is the largest coral atoll. Its reef measures 283 km (176 miles) long.

ISLAND ARC
On one side of a subduction zone, a curved chain or arc of volcanic islands may be pushed up from under the ocean floor. From space the numerous volcanic peaks on the islands of Indonesia are clearly visible.

THE WORLD'S LARGEST ISLANDS

ISLAND	AREA IN KM ^{2}	AREA IN MILES ^{2}
Greenland	2,175,219	839,852
New Guinea	792,493	305,981
Borneo	725,416	280,083
Madagascar	587,009	226,644
Baffin Island, Canada	507,423	195,916
Sumatra , Indonesia	427,325	104,990
Honshu, Japan	227,401	87,799
Great Britain	218,065	84,195

Sand builds up more on one side of the reef

New coral organisms grow on old coral skeletons

CORAL ISLAND

Islands such as the Maldives in the Indian Ocean are known as coral islands. Tiny marine organisms called corals grow on submerged rock formations such as undersea volcanoes (seamounts) in warm, salty seas. The coral grows slowly up to the ocean's surface and, when sea level drops, creates a firm platform above sea level.

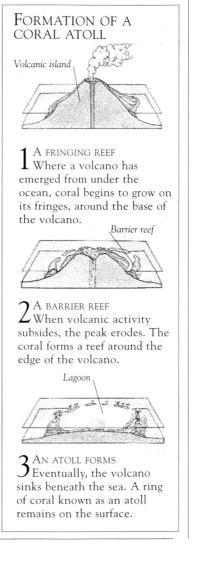

FORMATION OF A CORAL ATOLL

Volcanic island

1 A FRINGING REEF
Where a volcano has emerged from under the ocean, coral begins to grow on its fringes, around the base of the volcano.

Barrier reef

2 A BARRIER REEF
When volcanic activity subsides, the peak erodes. The coral forms a reef around the edge of the volcano.

Lagoon

3 AN ATOLL FORMS
Eventually, the volcano sinks beneath the sea. A ring of coral known as an atoll remains on the surface.

COASTS

WHERE THE LAND meets the sea there is the coast.
Coasts may have cliffs, or sandy or pebble beaches.
There is a continual battle between sea and coast
as rock is broken down by pounding waves, and
sand carried about by wind. Some coasts retreat
but new coast is always being deposited in other
areas. Beaches alter with the
seasons, as sand shifts along
the shore or out to sea.

*Longshore drift carries
sand across a bay or
river mouth*

*Waves slow at
the end of the tail
or spit of sand*

Sand spit

LONGSHORE DRIFT

*A pebble moves in a
zig-zagged path along the beach*

BEACH FORMATION
Sand and shingle deposited along
the shore form a beach. Its shape
is determined by the angle of the
waves. This process is called
longshore drift. Storms hurl beach
debris about, but eventually most
ends up on the seabed.

*Waves strike the
beach at an angle*

*Wind and
wave direction*

COAST FACTS

- The largest pleasure beach is Virginia Beach, U.S.A. with an area of 803 km² (310 miles²).

- The world has about 504,000 km (312,000 miles) of coastline.

- The highest sea cliffs are at Molokai, Hawaii. They descend 1,010 m (3,300 ft) to the sea.

- At Martha's Vineyard, U.S.A. the cliffs retreat 1.7 m (5.6 ft) per year.

Groynes or fences built into the sea prevent longshore drift

Sand builds up against the groyne

Sand and shingle

TYPES OF COAST

Direction of waves

TOMBOLO
This type of coastline links an island to the shore by a strip of sand.

BARRIER BEACH
A lagoon forms behind a barrier of sand built by onshore waves.

Direction of waves

BAYHEAD BEACH
Waves striking a headland at an angle leave a protected arc of sand.

FJORD COASTLINE
A submerged glacial valley with steep sides forms a fjord coastline.

SEA STACKS
Waves, carrying sand and pebbles, gradually wear away a headland. First, a cave appears, which is enlarged to form an arch. Then, the arch falls, leaving an isolated stack.

Sea cave eroded by sea until arch forms

Top of arch collapses leaving pillar or stack

113

RIVERS AND LAKES

THE WORLD'S RIVERS

WHEREVER THEY occur, rivers are a key part of the Earth's water cycle. They carry rainwater from high areas down to the sea, filling up lakes and pools on the way. In some parts of the world, rivers do not exist all year round. During the dry season they can disappear altogether but reappear once the wetter season begins.

PERENNIAL RIVER
In temperate and tropical areas a reliable supply of rainwater creates perennial rivers. Rivers such as the Nile, in Africa, flow all year round.

THE WATER CYCLE
Water is constantly circulating between land, sea, and air. The Sun's heat causes evaporation from seas, lakes, and rivers. Tiny droplets of water vapour rise and form clouds. The droplets cool and condense to fall as rain. The water fills rivers and lakes and flows to the sea.

Rain and snow fall on high ground

On land, water vapour is released by plants

RIVER FACTS
• The River Nile is longer, but the Amazon carries more water.

• China's Yangtze carries 1,600,000 tonnes (tons) of silt a year.

Water seeps underground and flows to sea

Water evaporates from sea and lakes to form clouds of water vapour

Rivers flow to the sea.

SEASONAL RIVER

This dry river bed belongs to a Spanish seasonal river. In the hot summer many rivers dry up, but during the wet winter season rain will fill them up.

THE WORLD'S LONGEST RIVERS

RIVER AND CONTINENT	LENGTH IN KM	LENGTH IN MILES
Nile, Africa	6,695	4,160
Amazon, S. America	6,437	4,000
Yangtze/Chang Jiang, Asia	6,379	3,964
Mississippi-Missouri, N. America	6,264	3,892
Ob-Irtysh, Asia	5,411	3,362
Yellow/Huang He, Asia	4,672	2,903
Congo/Zaire, Africa	4,662	2,897
Amur, Asia	4,416	2,744
Lena, Asia	4,400	2,734
Mackenzie-Peace, N. America	4,241	2,635

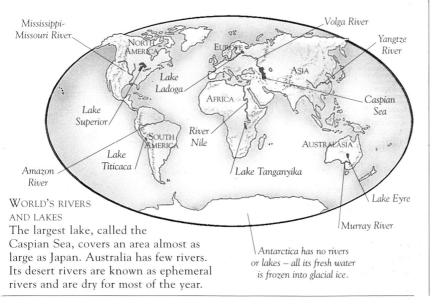

Mississippi-Missouri River

Volga River

Yangtze River

NORTH AMERICA

EUROPE

ASIA

Lake Ladoga

AFRICA

Lake Superior

Caspian Sea

SOUTH AMERICA

River Nile

AUSTRALASIA

Amazon River

Lake Titicaca

Lake Tanganyika

Lake Eyre

WORLD'S RIVERS AND LAKES

The largest lake, called the Caspian Sea, covers an area almost as large as Japan. Australia has few rivers. Its desert rivers are known as ephemeral rivers and are dry for most of the year.

Murray River

Antarctica has no rivers or lakes – all its fresh water is frozen into glacial ice.

117

RIVER FEATURES

FROM ITS SOURCE in the mountains, the snow or rainwater that fills a stream cuts a path through rock on its way to the sea. Streams join and form a river that flows more slowly, meandering across the land. A river may carry a large amount of sediment, which it deposits on the low, flat river valley and the floor of the sea.

DELTA
At the river's mouth, it sheds its sediment to form a broad fan of swampy land.

Streams may branch into channels or braids on the flood plain

Levee (raised bank)

Meander

Mountain stream

Steep gorge cut by the river

Oxbow lake

Natural bridge

RIVER FEATURES
As a river flows downhill it may carve a steep gorge through the rock. Downstream, the river moves from side to side in meanders, some of which may be isolated as oxbow lakes. On the flood plain, sediment left when the river floods builds levees.

Lake

River mouth

MELTWATER
A river may begin its life in a glaciated part of the world. Melting ice and snow from a glacier feed mountain streams.

OVERLAND FLOW
Rainwater running downhill gathers into small streams called tributaries, which join to form a river.

SPRING
A rock layer called the aquifer stores rainwater. The water may appear as a spring when the aquifer is near the surface.

MORE RIVER FACTS

• The Ganges and Brahmaputra delta, India, is the largest in the world. Its area is about 75,000 km² (30,000 miles²).

• The widest waterfall is Khone Falls in Laos. They are 10.8 km (6.7 miles) wide.

• Each year rivers unload 20,000 million tonnes (tons) of sediment into the sea.

Softer rock undercut by rock and water

Swirling rocks and water

Hard rock

Flood plain where sediment is deposited

Most rivers run into the sea

Sediment on seabed

WATERFALLS
A river flows swiftly near its source cutting through soft rocks more easily than hard. A sheer face of hard rock is exposed where water plunges, undercutting the rock below.

THE WORLD'S HIGHEST WATERFALLS

WATERFALL AND COUNTRY	HEIGHT IN METRES	HEIGHT IN FEET
Angel Falls, Venezuela	979	3,212
Tugela Falls, S. Africa	853	2,799
Utgaard, Norway	800	2,625
Mongefossen, Norway	774	2,539
Yosemite Falls, U.S.A.	739	2,425

LAKES

AN INLAND BODY of fresh water or salt water, collected in a hollow, is called a lake. In geological terms, lakes are short-lived; they can dry up or become clogged in a few thousand years. Lakes form when depressions resulting from crustal movement, erosion, or volcanic craters fill up with water. The Caspian Sea, in the former Soviet Union, the world's largest lake, and Lake Baikal, Siberia, the world's deepest lake, were both produced when the crust lifted, cutting off areas of the sea.

SWAMP
The Everglades, U.S.A are mangrove swamps. In warm climates, mangrove trees grow in the salty (brackish) water of muddy estuaries. The trees form islands in the mud.

TYPES OF LAKE

KETTLE LAKE
Melting glaciers leave behind ice blocks and debris. Melted ice fills depressions between the debris to form kettle lakes.

TARN
A circular mountain lake is known as a tarn. These lakes form in hollows worn by glacial erosion or blocked by ice debris.

VOLCANIC LAKE
The craters of ancient volcanoes fill up with water and produce lakes such as Crater Lake, Oregon, U.S.A.

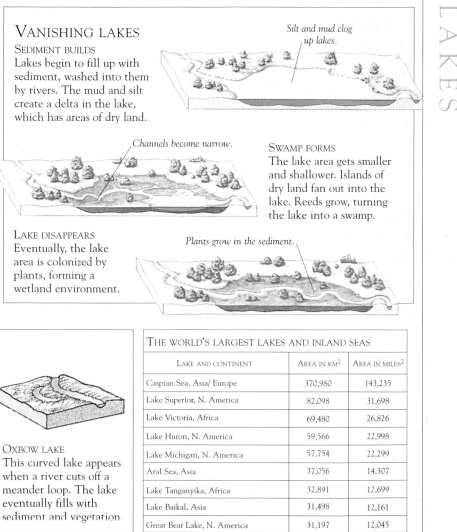

VANISHING LAKES

SEDIMENT BUILDS

Lakes begin to fill up with sediment, washed into them by rivers. The mud and silt create a delta in the lake, which has areas of dry land.

Silt and mud clog up lakes.

Channels become narrow.

SWAMP FORMS

The lake area gets smaller and shallower. Islands of dry land fan out into the lake. Reeds grow, turning the lake into a swamp.

LAKE DISAPPEARS

Eventually, the lake area is colonized by plants, forming a wetland environment.

Plants grow in the sediment.

OXBOW LAKE

This curved lake appears when a river cuts off a meander loop. The lake eventually fills with sediment and vegetation.

THE WORLD'S LARGEST LAKES AND INLAND SEAS		
LAKE AND CONTINENT	AREA IN KM²	AREA IN MILES²
Caspian Sea, Asia/ Europe	370,980	143,235
Lake Superior, N. America	82,098	31,698
Lake Victoria, Africa	69,480	26,826
Lake Huron, N. America	59,566	22,998
Lake Michigan, N. America	57,754	22,299
Aral Sea, Asia	37,056	14,307
Lake Tanganyika, Africa	32,891	12,699
Lake Baikal, Asia	31,498	12,161
Great Bear Lake, N. America	31,197	12,045

HARNESSING WATER

HUMANS CANNOT survive without water. As well as for drinking, fresh water is needed for crops and for industry. Rain may be stored in lakes, rivers, and reservoirs. Water's moving energy can be harnessed in hydroelectric power stations to produce electricity. It may be channelled to nourish plants and even provide waterways for boats. For domestic use water is cleansed, treated, and recycled.

IRRIGATION
Rice-terracing is a method of crop irrigation used in Indonesia. Growing rice requires a great deal of water. To make maximum use of rainfall, a system of channels carries water to the fields of rice. The fields are cut in layers down the hillsides.

CANALS
During the Industrial Revolution in Britain in the 1800s, a network of waterways called canals was constructed. Goods could be transported by barges that were pulled along by horses. Aqueducts carry canals and their traffic over obstacles.

Cleansing Water

Rainwater in lakes or reservoirs must be treated with chemicals before it can be used. In treatment plants, water passes through filter beds, chlorine gas, and other chemicals to remove impurities. In populated areas water goes through a constant cleansing cycle.

The chemicals aluminium sulphate and calcium hydroxide form a sticky substance to trap particles

A dam holds back water in a reservoir

Water is filtered by sand and gravel beds where dirt is trapped

Chlorine gas is bubbled through the water to kill bacteria

Dams

A dammed river like this one in California, U.S.A. can be used to produce hydroelectric power. Water held in a reservoir by a dam spins a turbine as it is released. The turbine is linked to a generator which produces electricity. Water above a waterfall can be diverted to drive an electrical generator.

Dam Facts

• Water held by Volta Dam in Ghana could flood 8,500 km² (3282 miles²).

• A chain of dams being built along the Amazon could flood an area the size of England.

• There are more than 200 dams around the world that are over 150 m (492 ft) tall.

CLIMATE AND WEATHER

CLIMATE

TYPICAL LONG-TERM weather conditions for an area are known as its climate. There are three broad climate zones: tropical, temperate, and polar. One factor that affects climate is distance from the equator (latitude). Different areas of the planet can share the same climate because they share the same latitude. The nearer the equator, the warmer the climate, and the nearer the poles, the colder. Distance from the sea and altitude also affect climate.

TEMPERATE GRASSLAND
The temperate climates of North America and Northern Europe have seasons and a pattern of seasonal rainfall.

MICROCLIMATE
In a city, such as Paris, the weather may differ from that of outlying areas. Roads and buildings absorb heat to create a local or microclimate.

TROPICAL RAINFOREST
The climate in regions of dense vegetation near the equator is hot and wet all year round. The temperature stays constant at about 80–82°C (27–28°F).

POLAR REGIONS AND TUNDRA REGIONS

At the ice-covered poles, temperatures only rise above freezing for a few months of the year. The cold, dry tundra region surrounds the north pole.

CLIMATE FACTS

• The temperature in the shade at al'Aziziyah, Libya of 58°C (136°F), is the highest recorded.

• Oymyakon in Siberia, the coldest inhabited place, can reach −68°C (−90° F).

MOUNTAIN REGIONS

The temperature falls the higher up a mountain you go. Trees and plants grow on the low slopes but little grows above the snowline.

MAP OF
CLIMATIC
ZONES

HOT DESERT

Few animals and plants can live in the hot, dry conditions of the desert. The temperature can reach 38°C (100°F) and it may not rain for several years.

KEY TO CLIMATIC ZONES

Polar

Tundra

Mountain

Temperate grassland

Tropical rainforest

Hot desert

WIND AND WEATHER

WINDS CIRCULATE air around the planet. They carry warm air from the equator to the poles and cold air in the opposite direction. This process balances the Earth's temperature. Some global winds (known as prevailing winds), such as polar easterlies and trade winds, are an important part of the world's weather systems.

Cold polar easterlies sink and spread to warmer areas

Warm air rises and spreads over cold air

Prevailing winds blow from the south-west

Trade winds

There is very little wind in the doldrums on the equator

Hot air moves away from the equator towards the poles, where it cools.

Prevailing winds blow from the north-west

Cold polar air

Cells of air circulate above the planet

WIND FACTS

• In Antarctica wind can reach speeds of 320 km/h (200 mph).

• Highest wind speed recorded at ground level is 371 km/h (230 mph).

WINDS OF THE WORLD
Three prevailing winds blow around the planet at ground level, on either side of the equator. Trade winds bring dry weather, westerly winds are damp and warm, and polar easterlies carry dry, cold polar air.

FORMATION OF A ROSSBY WAVE

A SNAKING WIND
The Earth's rotation causes curling, high altitude winds called Rossby waves.

DEEPENING WAVE
The wave deepens along the polar front. It forms a meander 2,000 km (1,250 miles) long.

DEVELOPED LOOPS
The curls become loops and the hot and cold air separate to produce swirling frontal storms.

Earth's rotation deflects winds on the ground

Trade winds near the equator

SEA BREEZES AND LAND BREEZES
On sunny days the land warms up during the day. Warm air rises from the land and cool air is drawn in from the sea. At night the land cools down quickly and cold air sinks out to sea.

DAYTIME
SEA BREEZE

Air rises over the relatively warm land

Cool air blows inland from the sea

Cool air sinks over the land

NIGHT-TIME
LAND BREEZE

Air rises over the relatively warm sea

TRADE WINDS
In the area either side of the equator (the tropics) the prevailing winds are called the trade winds. In the northern hemisphere the winds blow from the north-east, and in the southern hemisphere they blow from the south-east.

WEATHER MAPPING

MILLIONS OF PEOPLE listen to the weather forecast each day. The forecast is compiled using data collected from all around the world and even from weather satellites in space. Meteorologists study the movements of warm and cold air masses and the fronts where they meet. Using this information they plot weather charts and predict the coming weather.

SATELLITE IMAGES
From space, the Earth appears to be surrounded by swirling clouds. Africa's desert has no cloud cover.

WEATHER MAP
A picture of the weather at a given time can be shown on a weather map, known as a synoptic chart. Standard symbols are used, such as lines to show fronts (where one body of air – an air mass – meets another).

Occluded front – merged warm and cold front

A depression – a centre of low pressure

Closer isobars indicate stronger wind

Shows wind strength and direction

Cold front – cold air is advancing

Air pressure in millibars

Centre of high pressure

Warm front – warm air is advancing

Isobars link points with the same air pressure

FORMATION OF A DEPRESSION

AIR MASSES
Air masses are a vast area of wet or dry, warm or cold air. At the polar front, a warm air mass and a cold one collide.

FORMING A BULGE
The warm tropical air mass pushes into the cold polar air along the polar front. The front begins to bulge.

DIVIDING INTO TWO
The Earth's rotation spins the air masses. Cold air pursues warm air in a spiral formation. The polar front splits.

OCCLUDED FRONT
When the cold front catches up with the warm front, it pushes under the warm air. An occluded front results.

BAROMETER
The air around the Earth has mass and exerts pressure. A barometer measures air pressure in units called millibars.

TEMPERATURE PEAKS
This chart shows five ice ages in Earth's history, when the temperature fell and ice sheets covered much of the planet. These cold periods were separated by interglacials when the average temperature rose.

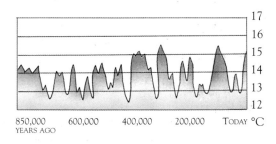

17
16
15
14
13
12

850,000   600,000   400,000   200,000   TODAY °C
YEARS AGO

CLOUDS

AIR RISES as it warms, as it passes over mountains, or when it is blown upwards by cool air. Rising air cools, condenses, and forms clouds of water droplets. There are three cloud levels: cirrus form at the highest level, alto in the middle, and stratus at the lowest level.

FOGGY AIR
Clouds that form at ground level are known as fog. Fog, mixed with smoke from burning fuels, produces smog. In 1952, London, England suffered from severe smog.

CLOUD FORMATION

THE LAND WARMS
The Sun warms the land on a clear day. Air near the ground is warmed and rises.

A CLOUD FORMS
As the warm air rises, it cools. The moisture it contains condenses and forms a cloud.

GROWING CLOUDS
Fleecy clouds appear in the sky. They get bigger and cool air circulates inside them.

OKTAS

Cloud cover is measured in oktas. On weather maps a partially shaded circle represents cover.

CLEAR   1   2

3   4   5   6   7   8

Freezing level

A
B
C
D
E
F
G
H
I

CLOUD TYPES

CIRRUS (A)
- wisps of cloud made of ice crystals
- about 12, 000 m (39,370 ft) high

CIRROCUMULUS (B)
- forms at about 9,000 m (29,528 ft)
- rippled ice crystal cloud

CUMULONIMBUS (C)
- dark, storm cloud with rain

ALTOCUMULUS (D)
- layers or rolls of fluffy cloud

ALTOSTRATUS (E)
- grey or white sheet of cloud
- forms between 2,000 m and 6,000 m (6,562 ft and 19,685 ft)

STRATOCUMULUS (F)
- layer at the top of cumulus cloud

CUMULUS (G)
- large, white, heaped, fluffy cloud

NIMBOSTRATUS (H)
- low, rain cloud
- under 2,000 m (6,562 ft)

STRATUS (I)
- low-level, flat, grey sheet of cloud

RAIN AND THUNDERSTORMS

EARTH'S WATER CYCLE relies on rain. Rain fills rivers and lakes and provides water for plants and animals. Tiny water droplets in the air form rain when they gather into larger drops inside clouds. Raindrops can be moved about by warm and cold air currents. Inside cumulonimbus clouds, droplets are tossed around until they produce the electric spark we know as lightning.

Droplets of more than 0.5 mm (0.02 in) fall as rain.

Smaller drops of water fall as drizzle.

Rising air

HOW RAIN FORMS
In tropical areas, rising air currents agitate the water droplets in clouds until they join into raindrops. In temperate regions, ice crystals in the clouds above freezing level melt on their way down and form rain.

MONSOON
Seasonal winds called monsoons draw moist air inland, bringing summer rain to southern Asia. In winter, a cold, dry wind blows over the land and out to the ocean.

RAIN FACTS

• A record 1,870 mm (73.62 in) of rain fell in one month in 1861 in Cherrapunji, India.

• Tutunendo, Colombia, the world's wettest place, has an annual rainfall of 11,770 mm (463.4 in).

LIGHTNING

Water droplets and ice in a storm cloud collide and build up electric charges. Positive charges gather at the top of the cloud and negative ones at the base. When the electricity is released it flashes between clouds or sparks to the ground and back again.

Positive charges

Negative charges

RAINBOWS

Sunlight striking raindrops is refracted, reflected by the backs of the droplets, and refracted again. This causes the white light to split into its seven constituent colours: red, orange, yellow, green, blue, indigo, and violet.

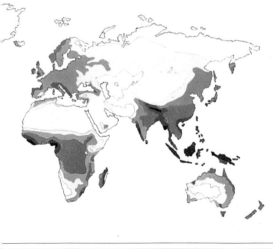

RAINFALL MAP

Around the world rainfall varies greatly. Warm seas in the tropics evaporate and bring lots of rain. Near the sea land is wetter but mountains may block rain.

KEY TO ANNUAL RAINFALL

○ Less than 250 mm (10 in)

○ 250–500 mm (10–20 in)

◔ 500–1,000 mm (20–39 in)

◕ 1,000–2,000 mm (39–79 in)

● 2,000–3,000 mm (79–118 in)

● More than 3,000 mm (118 in)

SNOW, HAIL, AND FROST

WHEN THE WEATHER is very cold, snow, hail, or frost leave a white coating on the landscape. Snow and hail fall from clouds. They are a result of water freezing in the cloud. Frost forms when water in the air condenses and freezes as it touches a cold surface. It leaves an icy glaze on windows, trees, and roads.

SNOWY WEATHER
In the European Alps the snow in the winter months does not melt because the ground temperature is low. Strong winds sometimes blow the snow into deep snowdrifts.

HOW SNOW FORMS
High up in the atmosphere, above the freezing level, water droplets in clouds form ice crystals, which collide and combine. As they fall, the ice crystals form snowflakes.

SNOW FACTS
• The largest recorded hailstone weighed 765 g (1.7 lb) and fell in Kansas, U.S.A. in 1970.

• In 1921, in Colorado, U.S.A., 1,930 mm (76 in) of snow fell in one day.

Some ice crystals melt on their way down, forming sleet.

Ice crystals which stay frozen fall as snow.

Rain

Warm air rising

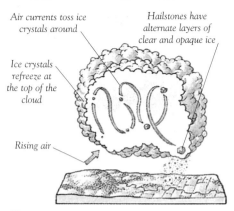

Air currents toss ice crystals around

Hailstones have alternate layers of clear and opaque ice

Ice crystals refreeze at the top of the cloud

Rising air

HOW HAIL FORMS

In cumulonimbus clouds above 10 km (6 miles) the temperature is freezing. Water droplets blown to the top of the cloud freeze. Layers of ice build up around the hailstone as it repeatedly melts and refreezes.

FROZEN RIVER

The Zanskar River in the Himalayas is frozen during the winter months. The frozen river makes travelling in the region easier, as local people can walk up and downstream on the ice. Under the ice fish can survive in the unfrozen water. In summer, the river is a fast-flowing torrent.

ICICLES

Spectacular ice shapes, such as icicles, form when water freezes in cold weather. Icicles grow as drips of melting snow or ice refreeze.

The outside of an icicle freezes before the inside

Icicles often hang from leaking pipes

HOAR FROST

Below freezing point, water vapour in the air freezes. It leaves spiky crystals of hoar frost on cold surfaces.

HURRICANES AND TORNADOES

WINDS SUCH AS hurricanes,(cyclones), and tornadoes occur when warm air masses encounter cold air masses. Winds reach high speeds and bring torrential rain and huge dark clouds. A tornado concentrates its havoc on a fairly narrow trail whereas a hurricane destroys a much larger area and can last for many days.

BEAUFORT SCALE	
NUMBER	DESCRIPTION
0	Calm, smoke rises straight up
1	Light air, smoke drifts gently
2	Light breeze, leaves rustle
3	Gentle breeze, flags flutter
4	Moderate wind, twigs move
5	Fresh wind, small trees sway
6	Strong wind, large branches move
7	Near gale, whole tree sways
8	Gale, difficult to walk in wind
9	Severe wind, slates and branches break
10	Storm, houses damaged, trees blown down
11	Severe storm, buildings seriously damaged
12	Hurricane, devastating damage

SATELLITE PHOTOGRAPH
Hurricanes can be tracked easily from space using satellites. The swirling clouds accumulate from tropical thunderstorms. They build into tight bands of spiralling clouds.

HURRICANE
Coasts, in particular, are damaged by hurricanes. Large waves are whipped up by the storms which lash coastlines and can cause floods.

Cirrus and cirrostratus clouds around the edge of the storm

Hurricanes can be as wide as 780 km (480 miles).

Bands of wind and rain spiral

At the eye the sky is clear and winds light

Currents rise and spread outwards

HOW A HURRICANE FORMS

A cluster of tropical storms can become a hurricane. Bands of cumulonimbus and cumulus clouds spiral towards the centre of the storm. Warm air rises and cools, building huge storm clouds that bring rain. At the centre, or eye, of the hurricane, the pressure is low and the weather is calm.

WATERSPOUT

If a tornado occurs over the ocean it is known as a waterspout. Water is sucked up in a column by winds reaching speeds of 80 km/h (50 mph), less than those of a tornado.

A violent updraught sucks up dust and vehicles

Winds in the tornado may reach speeds of 450 km/h (280 mph)

HURRICANE FACTS

• Winds up to 320 km/h (200 mph) have been recorded in a hurricane.

• Hurricanes spin anti-clockwise north of the equator and clockwise south of the equator.

• Waterspouts are usually between 50 and 100 m (164–328 ft) high.

TORNADO

If a mass of cool, dry air collides with a mass of warm, damp air it may form a tornado. This dark funnel of whirling air picks up debris from the ground. The storm may last only a few minutes but its spinning winds are very destructive.

A FUTURE FOR THE EARTH

ECOLOGY

THE STUDY OF the relationships between animals and plants, and between them and their environment, is called ecology. Ecology explains how individual species fit into the natural world. Ecologists study how organisms obtain food and materials to survive and the effect this has on the environment and on other organisms. Ernst Haekel, a German biologist, first used the term "ecology" in 1866.

ECOSYSTEMS
Several communities of living things, their physical surroundings and their climate make up an ecosystem. Beach, forest, and ocean communities are an example of ecosystems.

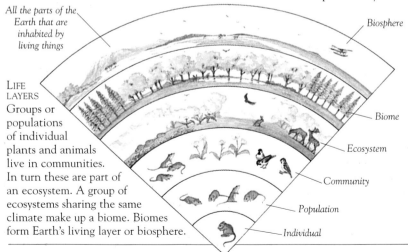

All the parts of the Earth that are inhabited by living things

Biosphere

LIFE LAYERS
Groups or populations of individual plants and animals live in communities. In turn these are part of an ecosystem. A group of ecosystems sharing the same climate make up a biome. Biomes form Earth's living layer or biosphere.

Biome

Ecosystem

Community

Population

Individual

FOOD WEB
Feeding relationships between organisms in an ecosystem can be complex. Energy, as food, is transferred along a chain from plants to plant eaters to meat eaters. Chains interconnect to build a food web.

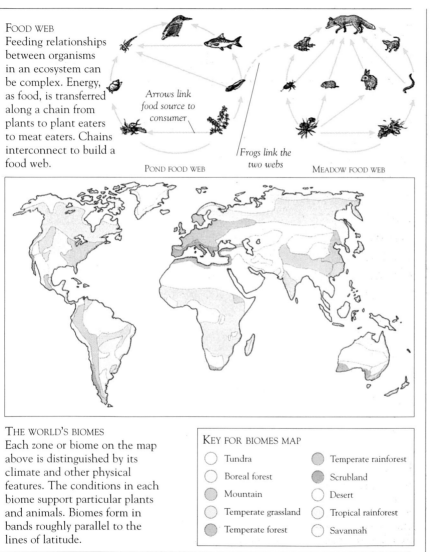

Arrows link food source to consumer

POND FOOD WEB

Frogs link the two webs

MEADOW FOOD WEB

THE WORLD'S BIOMES
Each zone or biome on the map above is distinguished by its climate and other physical features. The conditions in each biome support particular plants and animals. Biomes form in bands roughly parallel to the lines of latitude.

KEY FOR BIOMES MAP
- Tundra
- Boreal forest
- Mountain
- Temperate grassland
- Temperate forest
- Temperate rainforest
- Scrubland
- Desert
- Tropical rainforest
- Savannah

HABITAT DESTRUCTION

AS HUMANS SEEK a more comfortable life the Earth's resources are being used up or destroyed. Fossil fuels

are burned to provide energy and waste is dumped which pollutes land, sea, and air. Toxins that do not break down are left to poison the planet. Cultivating more and more land has led to the loss of habitats like the rainforest, endangering its many unique species. We need to protect the Earth – our own habitat – for our own survival.

DEFORESTATION
Forests are destroyed as people clear land for their animals, to grow crops, or to sell the wood. Deforestation leads to habitat and wildlife loss.

Oil spilt at sea is washed up on the beach.

WATER POLLUTION
Once in the water cycle, pollutants such as chemical waste, petrol, or oil can contaminate surface and ground water. Pollution of oceans and beaches kills animals and plants and poisons their habitats.

DESERTIFICATION
Land at the Sahara's edge is becoming desert. Over-grazing leaves fewer plants, causing soil erosion.

ACID RAIN

Burning fossil fuels releases carbon dioxide and sulphur dioxide into the atmosphere. These gases mix with rain making it acid. Acid rain damages some tree species and kills life in lakes near industrial areas.

Ozone hole shown in purple on this satellite image

OZONE HOLE

The ozone layer blocks out most of the Sun's harmful radiation. CFCs (chlorofluorocarbons), used in refrigerators, packaging, and aerosols may be causing a hole in the ozone layer over Antarctica.

More heat is reflected back to Earth

Less heat escapes

Gases trapped in Earth's atmosphere

Surface of the Earth gets hotter

GLOBAL WARMING

Polluting gases such as carbon dioxide are accumulating in the Earth's atmosphere. These gases, also known as greenhouse gases, prevent heat escaping from the surface of the planet and cause the temperature on Earth to rise, a process called global warming.

HABITAT DESTRUCTION

CONSERVATION

ENDANGERED wildlife can benefit from our attempts to protect the environment. Animals and plants need their habitats preserved. Some species can adapt to life in a different environment, but others need assistance from zoos, reserves, and botanical gardens. Less waste and less pollution will also protect our unique planet.

CAPTIVE BREEDING
Endangered species such as pandas are encouraged to breed in captivity. This practice helps maintain and increase animal numbers.

Foxes are a familiar sight in European gardens.

ADAPTING TO CHANGE
Animals such as foxes and raccoons have adapted to increased urbanization. Many now live in parks and gardens and scavenge for food in bins.

WILDLIFE RESERVES
One species becomes extinct every day through hunting or habitat destruction. However, in some parts of the world animals such as rhinos, zebras, and elephants are protected in wildlife reserves where they can live and breed in a protected and natural environment.

RECYCLING RUBBISH

An average family throws away two tonnes (tons) of rubbish every year. A large proportion of household waste such as organic matter, glass, paper, and metal all have good recycling potential. The remaining rubbish is mostly plastics and composite objects which are difficult to recycle.

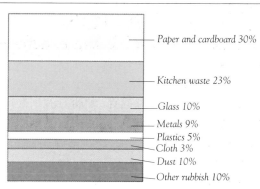

— Paper and cardboard 30%

— Kitchen waste 23%

—Glass 10%

— Metals 9%

— Plastics 5%

—Cloth 3%

— Dust 10%

—Other rubbish 10%

LAST WILDERNESS

Frozen Antarctica is a nearly deserted land, but the sea around it is teeming with life. Toxic dumping and mining are banned by an international convention in order to preserve Antarctica as Earth's last wilderness.

CONSERVATION FACTS

• Ingredients in some medicines, chocolate, and chewing gum were originally discovered in the rainforest.

• More than 68.5 per cent of coal's energy is lost on its way to providing energy for our homes.

• In the year 2000, California, U.S.A. generated 1.2 per cent of its electricity using wind turbines.

FUTURE ENERGY

Fossil fuels that are burnt to provide electricity will eventually run out. The Sun is a possible alternative energy source. Electric cars with solar panels are not yet practical but solar-powered telephones are already in use in some sunnier parts of the world.

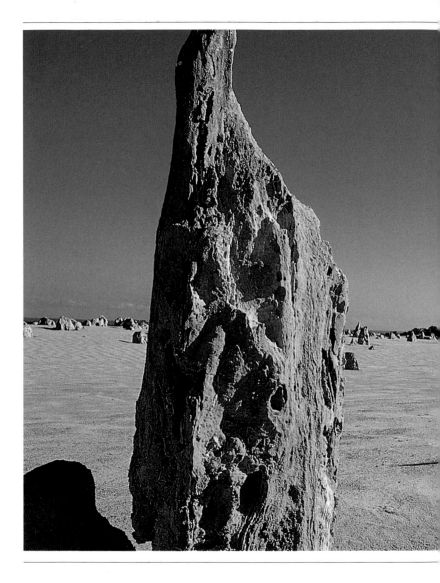

EARTH FACTS

PLANET EARTH

- With its oceans and swirling cloud, Earth is the most highly coloured planet in the solar system. Seen from space, it resembles a blue and white ball.

- Earth is the fifth-largest planet in the solar system, and is the densest of all the planets. Earth's density is five-and-a-half times the density of water.

- Earth's atmosphere contains enough water to cover the entire planet's surface to a depth of 2.5 cm (1 in). This has been calculated by satellites using infra-red technology.

Earth and Moon, as seen from the Gallileo spacecraft in 1992.

- Water covers more than two-thirds of the Earth's surface. Dry land occupies about 148,500,000 sq km (57,300,000 sq miles) of Earth's surface – about 29 per cent of the total surface area.

- The Sun's rays take about eight minutes to cover the 150,000,000 km (93,000,000 miles) from the Sun to the Earth.

THE MOON, EARTH'S SATELLITE

- The Moon orbits the Earth at a distance of about 385,000 km (238,860 miles). It is Earth's only natural satellite.

- At 3,476 km (2,160 miles) in diameter, the Moon is about one-quarter of Earth's size.

- Once or twice each year, the Moon's orbit positions it between the Sun and the Earth. It blocks the Sun's light, creating a shadow on Earth. This is called a solar eclipse.

- The Moon has no light of its own. Sunlight reflecting off its surface makes it shine. The light appears stronger at night.

- As it travels around the Earth once a month, the Moon appears to change shape. It remains the same shape, but the Sun lights different parts of it. From a tiny crescent, it seems to grow to a "full moon", and shrink back again. These transformations are called the phases of the Moon.

EARLY IDEAS

Early civilizations believed that the Earth lay at the centre of the universe.

- Greek philosopher Pythagoras (*c.* 582–497 B.C.) believed that the Earth lay in the centre of the universe. Transparent spheres orbited around the Earth at various distances, carrying the Sun, Moon, planets, and stars.

- Greek astronomer Aristarchus of Samos (*c.* 310–230 B.C.) was first to suggest that the Sun, not Earth, lay at the universe's centre, and that Earth orbited the Sun once a year. His ideas were not accepted at the time.

The Sun's surface, dotted with dark spots called sunspots

- In medieval Europe (*c.* A.D. 800–1500), Christian scholars believed that the world was a flat disc, surrounded by oceans. According to them, the city of Jerusalem lay at the centre of the universe.

- In 1530, the Polish astronomer Nicolaus Copernicus (1473–1543) suggested that the Earth moved around the Sun, which formed the centre of the solar system. For the next 300 years, the Catholic church banned Copernicus's book.

MILESTONES OF SPACE EXPLORATION

1957	The Soviet Union launches the first artificial satellite, Sputnik 1.
1959	Russian probe Luna 3 sends back the first pictures of the far side of the Moon.
1969	U.S. astronaut Neil Armstrong is the first man to set foot on the Moon.
1971	The first space station, Salyut 1, is launched to orbit Earth. The most recent space station was the International Space Station, launched in 2000.
1990	The Hubble Space Telescope is launched, and is repaired in space in 1993. It orbits the Earth at 600 km (375 miles).

The Hubble telescope circles the Earth about every 97 minutes.

FINDING OUT ABOUT THE EARTH

EARTH'S SHAPE AND SIZE

- Early civilizations such as the ancient Egyptians believed that the Earth was flat. The ancient Greeks were the first to study Earth's geography systematically.

- During the 6th century B.C., Greek scholar Pythagoras was among the first to maintain that the Earth was round. The philosopher Aristotle (384–322 B.C.) agreed, noticing that Earth cast a round shadow on the Moon during a lunar eclipse.

- Greek mathematician Eratosthenes (276–196 B.C.) managed to calculate Earth's circumference to within 80 km (50 miles) of the true figure.

- In 1525, French scholar Jean Fernel (1497–1558) produced a new, even more accurate figure for Earth's circumference.

- English scientist Isaac Newton (1642–1727) argued that Earth was not a perfect sphere, but bulged out at the Equator, and was flatter at the Poles. His theory was proved correct in the 1950s, when the first satellites took photographs of Earth from space.

EARTH'S STRUCTURE

- In the 4th century B.C., Aristotle suggested that the Earth was a solid ball of rock.

- In the 16th century, English physician William Gilbert (1544–1603) showed that the Earth was a giant magnet, which explained why compasses pointed north-south.

- In the late 18th century, a group of scientists called the Plutonists suggested that Earth's interior was molten rock, which erupted onto the surface through volcanoes.

- By the 1870s, most scientists believed that Earth had a solid central core, surrounded by an area of hot, fluid rock called the mantle, and an outer crust. This proved correct when the seismograph, an instrument for studying Earth's interior, was invented in 1880.

Statue of Aristotle at the Freiburg University, Germany.

STUDYING MOUNTAINS

- Before the 18th century, people believed that the Earth's surface and mountains were shaped by the Biblical flood.

- Scottish geologist James Hutton (1726–1797) suggested that mountains were shaped by weathering, uplift, and folding. He was later proved correct.

- British scientist George Airey (1801–1892) suggested that mountains rested on Earth's mantle, just as icebergs float in the ocean. His idea proved correct.

- U.S. professor James Dwight Dana (1813–1895) developed the shrinking Earth theory. He claimed that Earth's outer crust wrinkled and formed mountains as its hot core cooled, just as a drying apple's skin wrinkles. This was disproved in the 1950s.

- U.S. geologist Frank Taylor (1860–1939) argued that mountains form along the edges of continents as continents collide. The theory of plate tectonics later showed this idea to be correct.

The snow-covered peaks of Mount Rundle in the Rockies, Canada.

PLATE TECTONICS

- English philosopher Francis Bacon (1561–1626) noticed that on maps, the coasts of Africa and South America looked as if they would fit together. This suggested that they had once been joined.

- German explorer Alexander von Humboldt (1769–1859) noticed similarities between the rocks of Brazil in South America and the Congo in Africa.

- Mapping volcanoes and earthquakes around the Earth showed that the Earth's crust is divided into sections called "plates". These plates are constantly moving.

Ammonite fossil

- In 1962, U.S. geologist Harry Hess (1906–1969) suggested that the Atlantic Ocean floor is split in two and the two plates are moving apart.

- In the 1970s and 1980s, the theory of plate tectonics was developed, explaining the discoveries of identical rocks and fossils on continents now far apart.

EXPLORING THE EARTH

EXPLORING AUSTRALIA AND THE PACIFIC

FROM 40,000 B.C.   Groups of hunters from Asia use land bridges to reach and settle on the islands of Southeast Asia and Australia.

2000 B.C.–
A.D. 1000   Sailors from Southeast Asia explore and colonize the Pacific islands of Melanesia and Polynesia.

750s   The Maoris of Polynesia reach and colonize New Zealand.

1522   Spanish explorer Ferdinand Magellan completes the first voyage around the world.

1645   Dutchman Abel Tasman sails around Australia and sights New Zealand.

1768–1779   English explorer James Cook makes three voyages charting the South Pacific, including Tahiti and Australia.

1860–1861   An Australian expedition led by Robert Burke and William Wills is the first to cross Australia from south to north.

Ferdinand Magellan
(1480–1521)

MILESTONES IN MAP MAKING

- The first known map is a Babylonian tablet dating from 2300 B.C. It shows part of the state of Akkad in western Asia, with streams, hills, and compass points showing north, west, and east.
- Greek geographer Anaximander (610–546 B.C.) produced the first known world map, showing Greek lands surrounded by oceans.
- During the 3rd and 2nd centuries B.C., Greek scholars devised a grid of lines called latitude and longitude to divide Earth's surface. This allowed map-users to work out the distance between different locations.
- In 1552, Dutch map maker Gerardus Mercator (1512–1594) developed a new projection (the curved shape of the globe represented on a flat sheet of paper) for his world map. Mercator's projection is still widely used today.

EXPLORING THE AMERICAS

FROM 30,000 B.C.	Early people from Asia reach North America via a land bridge across the North Pacific. They spread south and reach the tip of South America by 9000 B.C.
A.D. 1000s	Vikings from Scandinavia reach the east coast of North America and establish a settlement there.
1492–1504	Italian explorer Christopher Columbus discovers the Americas on behalf of Spain.
1497	English explorer John Cabot reaches Newfoundland in Canada.
1519–1522	Spanish soldier Hernan Cortes explores and conquers the Aztec Empire in Mexico.
1607	English colonists establish the first permanent European settlement in North America.
1804–1806	American expedition led by Meriwether Lewis and William Clark reaches the Pacific coast.

EXPLORING AFRICA AND ASIA

1,500,000 B.C.	From Africa, humans spread to colonise Earth.
2600 B.C.–300 B.C.	Mediterranean peoples explore beyond their shores to parts of Africa, Europe, and western Asia.
A.D. 100s	Chinese traders establish the "Silk Road" trade route from China across Asia to the Mediterranean.
600s–750	Arabs explore and conquer a vast empire in North Africa and Spain, and in western Asia.
1271–1295	Italian explorer Marco Polo visits China.
1325–1354	Arab scholar Ibn Battuta travels widely in Africa and western Asia.
1404–1433	Chinese sea captain Cheng Ho sails on seven voyages of exploration around the Indian Ocean.
1511	Portuguese sailors reach the East Indies in southeast Asia.
1870s	Welsh reporter Henry Morton Stanley explores central Africa.

Statue of Christopher Columbus in Barcelona, Spain

VOLCANIC ERUPTIONS

LEGENDS ABOUT VOLCANOES

- Volcanoes are named after Vulcan, Roman god of fire and a blacksmith. His forge was thought to lie under Mount Etna in Sicily, in the Mediterranean. When Mount Etna spat fire, Vulcan was busy at his forge.

- Long ago, the Irish believed that a giant built the volcanic basalt pillars called the Giant's Causeway, by the Irish Sea, to attack another giant across the water.

- The people of the Hawaiian islands believed that their fire goddess, Pele, caused volcanic eruptions on the islands. Whenever a volcano rumbled, Pele was dancing.

- Japan's highest volcano, Mount Fuji, is a sacred mountain. The snowy cone was believed to be the home of the goddess Sengen-Sama. She guarded the mountain, which contained the sacred waters of life.

Japanese drawing of Mount Fuji

EFFECTS ON CLIMATE

Volcanic eruptions can have a far-reaching effect on the world's climate.

- Powerful eruptions send a cloud of ash high into the atmosphere, where it spreads on the wind. The ash can prevent sunlight from reaching Earth, causing temperatures to fall for days, months, or even years.

- Volcanic ash high in the atmosphere causes spectacular sunrises and sunsets. In the early 19th century, English painter JMW Turner painted a series of dramatic sunsets. They are now thought to have been caused by the eruption of Mount Tambora, Indonesia, in 1815.

- Carbon dioxide (CO_2) is one of the gases released during volcanic eruptions. Increased levels of CO_2 in the air, caused partly from volcanoes and also from pollution, are causing global warming.

- Sulphur dioxide, another gas released during eruptions, mixes with water vapour high in the atmosphere to form a weak acid. This then falls as acid rain.

INVESTIGATING VOLCANOES

Scientists called volcanologists use various techniques and equipment to study volcanoes and try to predict when they will erupt.

Protective mask for exploring volcanoes

- Laser beams are used to monitor the exact shape of volcanoes. Changes such as bulges appearing on a volcano's flank are a sign that the mountain may be about to erupt.

- Volcanologists collect samples of molten rock and gases from volcano craters. The samples may give clues about a volcano's activity.

- Scientists use electric thermometers called thermocouples to measure the temperature of molten rock. Some lava flows reach temperatures of over 1000°C (1800°F).

- Volcanologists wear fireproof clothing, helmets, and asbestos gloves to protect themselves from heat and toxic gases when studying volcanoes at close range.

VIOLENT ERUPTIONS

- In 1470 B.C., an eruption on the Greek island of Thira (now Santorini) sent a tidal wave racing across the ocean. It swamped the cities of the Minoan civilization on the nearby island of Crete.
- The 1883 eruption of Mount Krakatoa in Indonesia caused the loudest sound ever recorded. The explosion was heard on islands in the Indian Ocean 4,800 km (3,000 miles) away.
- In 1902, the eruption of Mount Pelée on the Caribbean island of Martinique killed everyone in the nearby town of St Pierre – except one man, Ludger Sylbaris. He was imprisoned in the local gaol, which saved him from the blast.
- In 1943, a farmer saw steam rising from his field near Paracutin, Mexico. It was the birth of a new volcano. Mount Paracutin is now a mountain over 2,700 m (8,850 ft) high.
- In 1986, an eruption beneath Lake Nios in Cameroon, West Africa, released a cloud of poisonous carbon dioxide gas. The deadly gas killed 1,700 people in villages nearby.

EARLY IDEAS ABOUT EARTHQUAKES

- According to Hindu mythology, the Earth rests on eight giant elephants. The elephants are balanced on a great turtle, which in turn stands on a cobra. Whenever any of the animals moves, the Earth shakes.

An illustration of the Hindu myth about how earthquakes occur.

- In ancient Japan, people believed that a giant catfish called the *namazu* lived in the mud under Earth's surface. When the catfish wriggled, an earthquake struck.

- The ancient Greeks were the first to offer natural causes as a scientific explanation for earthquakes. Aristotle believed that earthquakes struck when strong winds fanned the flames of fires deep inside the Earth.

EARTHQUAKE DISCOVERIES

- In the 19th century, Irish engineer Robert Mallet (1810–1881) drew up a world map to show the sites of earthquakes. It showed that earthquakes occurred only in certain regions, such as the "Ring of Fire" in the Pacific Ocean.

- In 1835, English naturalist Charles Darwin (1809–1892) noticed that a section of coastline in South America had risen upwards during an earthquake.

- Darwin's observations about blocks of land shifting during earthquakes were confirmed during an earthquake in Alaska in 1899.

- In 1935, U.S. geologist Charles Richter (1900–1985) devised his scale for measuring earthquakes. Italian scientist Giuseppe Mercalli produced his scale in 1931.

- During the late 20th century, the theory of plate tectonics explained why most earthquakes occur along the edges of the giant plates that make up Earth's crust. The earthquakes are caused by collisions between plates.

WORK OF SEISMOLOGISTS

- The world's first earthquake detector was invented by Chinese scholar Chang Heng in the 2nd century A.D. It was a brass jar containing a pendulum, and four brass dragons' heads holding balls. The vibrations of an earthquake caused the balls to drop into the mouth of a brass frog below.

- Modern seismologists (scientists who study earthquakes) use a variety of instruments to monitor and measure movement of the Earth.

- In earthquake-prone regions, scientists use laser beams to measure the slightest movement in rocks, which might give advance warning of a major earthquake.

- Scientists also measure the time intervals between earthquakes. They then use computers to predict when the next earthquake is due.

Equipment used by seismologists to monitor earth movement.

DESTRUCTIVE QUAKES

- The 1755 Lisbon earthquake started many fires in ruined buildings in the city. In the harbour, the sea drained away, then returned as a tidal wave.

- In 1963, a minor earthquake caused a landslide into a lake behind the Vaiont Dam in Italy. A wall of water leapt over the dam and crashed down to destroy villages below.

- In 1970, an earthquake in Peru started an avalanche on Mount Huascaran in the Andes. The melted snow, rock, and mud engulfed the town of Yungay in the valley, and 50,000 people died.

- In 1985, an earthquake caused the ground under Mexico City to turn boggy. Skyscrapers and the city's main hospital collapsed or sank into the mud.

- The Armenian earthquake of 1988 destroyed Leninakan, the country's second largest city.

Earthquake devastation in Istanbul, Turkey, in 1999.

NATURAL WONDERS

LANDMARKS OF EUROPE AND ASIA

- The Matterhorn, 4,478 m (14,690 ft) high, is a spectacular steep-sided mountain in the Alps, between Switzerland and Italy. It was shaped by glaciers on different sides of the mountain wearing the rock away.

- The Yarlung Zangbo Valley in eastern Tibet is thought to be the world's deepest valley. This 5,075 m (16,650 ft) chasm was caused by the Yarlung Zangbo River cutting deep into the Himalayan Mountains.

- Durdle Door in Dorset and the Green Bridge of Wales in Pembrokeshire are spectacular chalk arches on the coast that have been carved by the action of the waves.

WONDERS OF THE AMERICAS

- Rainbow Bridge in Utah, U.S.A., is the world's largest natural arch, 82 m (270 ft) long and 88 m (290 ft) high. It is made of sandstone rock sculpted by natural forces, including the wind.

- The Pantanal in Brazil, South America, is the world's largest wetland, covering 109,000 sq km (42,000 sq miles).

- Lake Titicaca, which lies between Peru and Bolivia in the Andes Mountains, is the world's highest navigable lake. It is 3,800 m (12,500 ft) above sea level.

- The world's highest waterfall, the Angel Falls in Venezuela, was named by U.S. pilot Jimmie Angel (1899–1956). The waterfall is 979 m (3,212 ft) high.

- The Grand Canyon, in Colorado, U.S.A., the world's largest gorge, is about 450 km (270 miles) long, 16 km (10 miles) wide and nearly 2 km (1 mile) deep. This giant cleft has been worn away by the Colorado River over six million years.

Famous chalk arch at Durdle Door in Dorset, southern England.

SPECTACULAR AFRICA

- The Great Rift Valley that stretches 4,000 km (2,500 miles) across East Africa is formed as two of the Earth's tectonic plates are moving apart, leaving a huge, flattish valley.

- The spectacular Victoria Falls, 108 m (355 ft) high, lie on the border between Zambia and Zimbabwe in east Africa. The waterfalls' local name, *Mosi oa Tunya*, means "Smoke that Thunders".

- The flat top of Table Mountain in Cape Town, South Africa, was created by centuries of erosion wearing away the sandstone rock.

- The Ngorongoro Crater in Tanzania, East Africa, is the caldera (crater) of an extinct volcano. The largest of its kind in the world, the crater is now a wildlife park.

- The Ahaggar Mountains in Algeria, North Africa, are a range of craggy peaks on the edge of the Sahara Desert. They are made of volcanic rock which cracked as it cooled, and gave the mountains a ribbed surface.

WONDERS OF AUSTRALIA

- The Devil's Marbles in the north Australian desert are a group of unusual round rocks. Their outer layers have peeled away because of the extreme temperatures in the desert.

- The Olgas are a group of curious, red, rounded rocks in central Australia. Their Aboriginal name, *Kata Tjuta*, means "Many Heads".

- *Uluru* (Ayers Rock) in central Australia is a giant red rock in the middle of a barren plain. With a circumference of 9 km (5.5 miles) and standing 350 m (1,140 ft) tall, it is the world's largest monolith (single rock). *Uluru* is sacred to the

Devil's Marbles, Australia

Aboriginal people. Its name means "great pebble".

- The Great Barrier Reef stretches for 2,030 km (1,260 miles) off the coast of northeastern Australia. The world's largest living organism, it is formed by tiny sea creatures called coral polyps.

SPACE MISSILES

WHAT ARE METEORS AND METEORITES?

- Meteors are bits of rock and dust from space that fall to Earth. They are called meteorites when they land on Earth's surface. Meteorites play a part in shaping Earth's landscape.

- Most meteors are tiny specks of dust that burn up in the atmosphere before reaching Earth. This produces streaks of light called shooting stars. Sometimes large numbers of shooting stars all fall at once – a meteor shower.

- On average, over a million meteors enter Earth's atmosphere each day. Most are no larger than a grain of sand.

- A few meteors are large enough to survive the trip through the atmosphere. As meteorites, they smash onto the planet's surface, gouging a huge impact crater in the ground.

- Most meteorites fall harmlessly into the oceans, but there are at least 150 huge craters around the world, where meteorites have crashed on to dry land.

METEORITE CRATERS

- Barringer Crater in Arizona, U.S.A., is a huge impact crater 1,250 m (4,150 ft) wide and 180 m (600 ft) deep. Scientists believe that a million-ton meteorite crash-landed here about 25,000 years ago.

- An enormous impact crater formed on the coast of the Yucatan Peninsula in Mexico when an asteroid crashed down 65 million years ago.

- About 65 million years ago, many of Earth's species, including the dinosaurs, suddenly died out. Some scientists believe the Yucatan asteroid may have caused the extinctions, by raising a dust cloud that blotted out the sun.

- Huge impact craters are also visible on the Moon, Mars, and other bodies in the solar system. The Moon has no atmosphere to burn up meteorites, so many crash-land there. One of the Moon's biggest craters is called Copernicus. It is 93 km (58 miles) in diameter.

The crater Daedalus on the far side of the Moon, as seen from the Apollo 11 spacecraft in 1969.

INVESTIGATING METEORITES

- The records of the ancient Egyptians, Greeks, Romans, and others contain many accounts of "stones from heaven". The Romans and Chinese believed that meteorites were sent by the gods.

- In the 18th century, German scientist Ernst Chladni (1756–1827) suggested that meteorites were the debris from planets, but his idea was ridiculed at the time.

- In 1803, the village of L'Aigle in France was hit by a shower of 3,000 small meteorites. French scientists analysed the rocks and some realised that they were material from space.

- Scientists now believe that meteorites are fragments of comets, asteroids, planets, or other bodies in space.

- Meteorites are classified according to their composition. There are three main types of meteorites: those made of stone, of iron, or a mixture of the two.

Asteroid

METEORITE FALLS AND FINDS

- In 1908, a huge meteorite exploded about 8 km (5 miles) above the ground in a remote part of Siberia in northern Russia. It left no crater, but it flattened trees over a wide area, and sent shock waves around the world.

- The world's largest known meteorite was found in Namibia, Africa, in 1920. It was 2.7 m (9 ft) long and 2.4 m (8 ft) wide. It weighed about 54 tonnes (53 tons) – as much as ten African elephants.

- In 1947, the town of Vladivostok in Russia was showered by a swarm (group) of meteorites, which left 106 craters up to 28 m (92 ft) deep.

- The greatest recorded meteor shower occured in 1966 above the Pacific. Around 2,000 meteors a minute streaked across the sky for 20 minutes – a total of 40,000 shooting stars.

Meteorite with its surface pitted by heat as it fell from space.

EARTH'S RICHES

EARTH'S GEOLOGY

- In 1650, Irish Archbishop James Ussher used the Bible to work out that the world began in 4004 B.C.

- Scottish geologist James Hutton (1726–1797) was among the first to argue that the Earth had been shaped gradually by natural forces.

- English engineer William Smith (1769–1839) realised that fossils found in rock could be used to establish the rock's age.

- French anatomist Georges Cuvier (1769–1832) founded the science of palaeontology – the study of fossils. He used fossilized bones to work out what a prehistoric animal had looked like.

- Many fossil and other geological discoveries have been made through mining and quarrying. In 1878, 30 complete Iguanodon skeletons were discovered in a coal mine in Bernissart, Belgium. These fossils showed exactly what this dinosaur had looked like.

MINING RECORDS

- The world's deepest gold mine is Western Deep Levels of Carletonville, South Africa. Begun in 1957, it is now 3,580 m (11,750 ft) deep. South Africa is the world's largest gold miner: 522 tonnes (512 tons) per year.

- The single most productive gold mine in the world is thought to be at Kyzyl Kum, in Uzbekistan, Asia. The mine yields an estimated 80 tonnes (78 tons) of gold each year.

- The world's oldest mine is a chert (silica) mine in Egypt, dating from 100,000 B.C.

- The world's deepest coal mine lies at Donbas field in the Ukraine. An exploratory shaft there descends 2,040 m (6,700 ft).

- The world's largest oil field is the Ghawar field in Saudi Arabia. The field is 240 km (150 miles) long and 35 km (22 miles) wide.

Fossilized lower jaw bone from a Gorgosaurus

RECORD-BREAKING GEMSTONES

- The world's largest uncut diamond, the Cullinan, was found in Pretoria, South Africa, in 1905. It was cut to make two major diamonds, called the Great Star of Africa and the Second Star of Africa, which are both part of the British Crown Jewels.

- The world's largest cut diamond is Unnamed Brown, owned by the South African mining company, De Beers. Weighing in at 545 carats, it is even larger than the famous Cullinan diamonds.

- The world's largest piece of opal was found at Coober Pedy, a famous opal-mining region in Australia. Weighing 26,350 carats, it is named Jupiter-Five.

- The world's largest star ruby weighs 6,465 carats. Probably found in India, it is called the Eminent Star.

- The world's largest pearl was found in the shell of a giant clam off the coast of the Philippines in 1934. Weighing 6.4 kg (14 lb), it is called The Pearl of Lao-tse.

*An example of
a star ruby*

MINING DISASTERS

- Britain's worst mining disaster occurred in Senghenydd Colliery in Wales in 1913. An explosion in the mine killed 439 people.

- At Honkeiko Colliery in China in 1942, a coal dust explosion killed 1,549 people. It was the worst mining disaster ever recorded.

- In 1966, a coal waste heap above the village of Aberfan in Wales collapsed after heavy rain. It engulfed the local school, and killed 28 adults and 116 children.

- In 1988, the Piper Alpha oil rig off the Scottish coast was rocked by explosions, which ignited the oil platform and the sea around it. Despite rescue efforts, 167 of the rig's crew died.

- In 1995, the lift in the Vaal Reefs Goldmine in South Africa plunged 490 m (1,600 ft), killing 105 miners.

RIVERS, MOUNTAINS, AND CAVES

EXPLORING GREAT RIVERS

- South America's greatest river, the Amazon, was first explored by Spanish soldier Francisco de Orellana (1511–1546), in 1540–1542.

- In 1682, French explorer René de La Salle (1643–1687) was first to travel the length of the Mississippi, North America's longest river.

- The River Niger in West Africa was first explored by Scottish doctor Mungo Park (1771–1806) in 1804–1806. However, Park drowned in the river without finding its source.

- British missionary and explorer David Livingstone (1813–1873) travelled the length of the mighty Zambezi River in east Africa to cross the African continent in 1854–1856.

- British explorer John Speke (1827–1864) tracked the source of Africa's longest river, the Nile, to Lake Victoria in 1858.

Statue of David Livingstone from the Royal Geographic Society, London

SCIENTIFIC IDEAS ABOUT RIVERS

- Before the 17th century, no-one understood why rivers kept flowing. They were thought to be fed from the sea via underground springs.

- In 1674, French scientist Claude Perrault (1613–1688) measured rainfall in the valley of the River Seine in France and realised that enough rain fell to feed the river.

- Dutch scientist Nicolaus Steno (1638–1686) was among the first to realise that hills were eroded by streams and rivers. They carried sediment from the hills downstream to the sea, where it settled to form new layers of rock.

- In 1875, U.S. explorer and geologist John Wesley Powell (1834–1902) conducted a pioneering study of the Colorado River in western U.S.A. He showed how the river had transformed the landscape there and formed the Grand Canyon.

  - At about the same time, U.S. geologist James Croll (1821–1890) studied the Mississippi River and realised that it carried huge amounts of sediment into the ocean.

MOUNTAINS AND MOUNTAINEERS

- Mont Blanc, Europe's highest mountain at 4,807 m (15,800 ft), was first climbed by French doctor Michel-Gabriel Paccard and guide Jacques Balmat in 1786.

- The world's highest mountain, Mount Everest, was first climbed by New Zealander Edmund Hillary (1919–) and Sherpa Tenzing Norgay (1914–1986) in 1953. The first woman to stand on Everest's summit was Japanese climber Junko Tabei (1939–), in 1975. The mountain is 8,848 m (29,028 ft) high.

- The highest mountain on an island is Puncak Jaya in Indonesia, which is 4,884 m (16,023 ft) high.

- The tallest mountain on the Equator is Mount Cayambe in Ecuador, which is 5,790 m (18,996 ft) high.

- Italian climber Reinhold Messner (1944–) was the first person to scale all 14 of the world's highest peaks, which are all over 8,000 m (26,250 ft) high. Messner achieved his remarkable feat without using oxygen.

CAVES AND CAVERS

- The world's largest cave is Sarawak Chamber on the island of Sarawak in Malaysia. It is 700 m (2,300 ft) long, about 300 m (980 ft) wide, and at least 70 m (230 ft) high.

- Excavations of the world's longest cave system, the Mammoth Cave System in Kentucky, U.S.A., have shown that the caves were used by humans 4,000 years ago.

- The world record for cave descent was made in the world's deepest cave, Jean Bernard Cave in France, in 1989. It is 1,602 m (5,256 ft) deep.

- The world's longest underwater cave lies in Mexico. Divers have so far mapped 40 km (25 miles) of passages, and exploration is still going on.

Stalactites and stalagmites in a cave in Carlsbad Caverns National Park, New Mexico.

EARTH FACTS

NAVIGATING THE OCEANS

- The ancient Greeks knew how to use the angle of the Sun at midday to calculate their longitude (distance east or west), but this method could not be precise until the invention of accurate clocks in the 1720s.

- At night, ancient Greek navigators used the Pole Star, which always shines in the north, to work out their latitude (distance north or south). Medieval sailors measured the Pole Star's height above the horizon using an astrolabe, a forerunner of the modern sextant.

- By the 12th century mariners were using magnetic compasses to calculate direction.

- Modern sailors use radar, radio, and satellites to chart their position precisely.

Astrolabe

Sextant – measures the altitudes of stars to determine a position on Earth.

EXPLORING THE OCEANS

- The history of scientific marine exploration dates from the 17th century, when the British scientific institution, the Royal Society, commissioned the first systematic study of the oceans.

- In 1724, Italian geologist Liugi Marsili (1658–1730) produced the first known chart of the seafloor.

- In 1855, U.S. naval officer Matthew Maury (1806–1873) charted the floor of the Atlantic Ocean, and published the first detailed study of the oceans, *The Physical Geography of the Sea*.

- In 1872–1876, the British research ship *Challenger* conducted the first thorough study of the world's oceans. In the course of its three-and-a-half-year voyage, the vessel visited every ocean except the Arctic. It mapped reefs and coastlines, and identified many new types of marine life.

- In the 1960s and 1970s, the Deep Sea Drilling Project, funded by six countries, collected samples from the seafloor of oceans worldwide. The drilling ship *Glomar Challenger* was used to collect the samples.

FINDING OUT ABOUT OCEANS

- In the 17th century, English scientist Isaac Newton (1642–1727) explained how the pull of the Moon's gravity on Earth helped to produce ocean tides.

- In the late 18th century, American scientist and politician Benjamin Franklin (1706–1790) conducted a study of currents in the Atlantic Ocean, and discovered the warm current known as the Gulf Stream.

- During World War I (1914–1918), French, German, British, and U.S. scientists developed sonar equipment, which uses pulses of sound to map the seafloor. In 1925, the German research ship *Meteor* used sonar soundings to chart the world's longest undersea mountain chain, the Mid-Atlantic Ridge.

- During the 1950s, U.S. scientist Maurice Ewing (1906–1974) discovered that the centre of the ocean floor in the Atlantic was made up of very young rocks. This suggested that the ocean floors were still spreading.

- In the 1960s, U.S. geologist Harry Hess (1906–1969) suggested that ocean floors spread out from mid-ocean ridges. This was later proved correct.

SUBMARINE EXPLORATION

The history of submarine exploration dates back as far as the fourth century B.C., when Greek general Alexander the Great (356–323 B.C.) had a diving bell made.

1775　American inventor David Bushnell (1742–1824) builds one of the first submarines, the *Turtle*.

1819　German inventor Augustus Siebe (1788–1872) develops a successful diving suit. Oxygen was supplied to the helmet from a ship on the surface.

1934　U.S. naturalists Charles Beebe and Otis Barton achieve a record-breaking dive, 775 m (2,500 ft) below sea level, in a new type of submarine called a bathysphere.

1943　French diver Jacques Cousteau (1910–1997) pioneers the aqualung, which uses cylinders of compressed air strapped to the diver's back.

1953　Swiss scientist Auguste Piccard (1884–1962) develops a submarine called a bathyscaphe to explore the deep oceans.

Turtle submarine

F O R E S T S

FORESTS OF THE WORLD

- Forests are an invaluable natural resource. They provide a home to over half of all land animals and insects.

- There are three main types of forests: coniferous, deciduous, and tropical. Climate is the biggest factor that decides which type of forest grows.

- Coniferous forests grow mainly in cold regions in the Northern Hemisphere. Tropical forests grow on either side of the Equator. Deciduous forests are mainly found in the temperate (mild) regions in between.

- The higher a forest's altitude (height above sea level), the wider the ranges of temperature. This affects which species of trees grow there.

CONIFEROUS FORESTS

- Most coniferous or cone-bearing trees are evergreen – they keep their leaves all year round.

- A broad belt of coniferous forest about 800 km (500 miles) wide runs right across northern Europe, Asia, and North America. It is called the taiga. The taiga makes up one third of the world's total forest area.

- Spruce and fir are the most common trees found in the taiga.

- In the taiga, winters are long and cold, summers are short and cool. In winter, trees continue to provide shelter for the animals of the forest, including lynx and wolves.

FOREST STRUCTURE

From the tops of the tallest trees to the ground, forests contain five distinct layers of vegetation, known as stories. The topmost storey of the forest is a dense leafy layer called the canopy. Below that is the understorey, made up of shorter trees. Next comes a storey of shrubs and bushes, then a layer of grass and flowers, and finally, the forest floor.

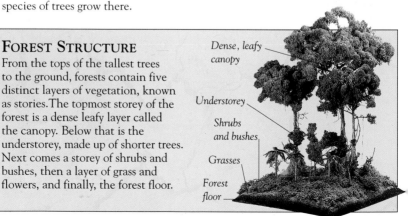

Dense, leafy canopy

Understorey

Shrubs and bushes

Grasses

Forest floor

DECIDUOUS FORESTS

- Deciduous forests cover a total of about 17 million sq km (6.5 million sq miles) – about 12 per cent of Earth's total land area.

- Deciduous (broad-leaved) trees shed their leaves in autumn, and grow new leaves in spring. The fallen leaves help to fertilize the forest soil.

- Deciduous forests once covered much of the temperate zone in the northern hemisphere, in North America, Europe, and eastern Asia. However, many of these ancient forests have now been felled.

- Deciduous trees also grow in parts of Africa, Asia, Australia, and South America which are close to the Equator and experience a monsoon (wet) season and a dry season each year. Broad-lived trees here shed their leaves in the dry season, and grow new ones at the start of the monsoon.

Deciduous tree

TROPICAL FORESTS

- In low-lying areas near the Equator, tropical forests receive 200–500 cm (80–200 in) of rain annually. In these warm, wet conditions, trees can grow 5 m (15 ft) a year.

- Tropical forests cover less than six per cent of Earth's land area, yet they contain over half of all the species of plants and animals in the world.

- Over half of the world's tropical forest lies in the Amazon region of South America. Africa, Southeast Asia, and Central America also have major tropical forests.

- Very little sunlight filters through the dense canopy of the tropical forest to reach the ground. When rain falls, it takes about ten minutes to drip through the leaves to the forest floor.

Tropical forest, New Zealand

DESERTS AND GRASSLANDS

DESERT LANDSCAPES

- Deserts cover roughly 25 per cent of Earth's dry land. Because they are so barren, only about five per cent of the world's population live there.

- Most people think of deserts as sandy, but only about 20 per cent of the world's deserts are actually sand-covered. The rest are mainly rocky or stony. In some, the ground is covered with salt or even ice.

- The Atacama Desert in Chile, South America, is the driest place on Earth. Rain has not fallen in some parts of the Atacama for several hundred years.

- Plants survive in deserts by developing very deep or long roots that gather moisture from a wide area. Succulents (desert plants such as cacti) store water in their fleshy leaves, stems, or roots.

Desert Saguaro cactus

DESERTS OF THE WORLD

- The world's largest desert is the Sahara Desert in North Africa. It covers 9,000,000 sq km (3,500,000 sq miles), roughly the same area as the U.S.A. Daytime temperatures in the Sahara can climb up to 55°C (130°F).

- The world's second-largest desert, which covers central Australia, is often broken down into smaller deserts, including the Gibson, Simpson, and Great Sandy Desert. In Australia, barren, scrubby land is also known as the Outback.

- The Arabian Desert in southwest Asia is the world's third-largest, covering 1,300,000 sq km (502,000 sq miles). Its dunes rise to 240 m (790 ft) high.

- The Gobi Desert in central Asia lies at 1,000 m (3,500 ft) above sea level. Its high altitude means that temperatures may climb to 50°C (122° F) during the day, but may fall to –40°C (–40°F) at night.

- Death Valley, California, U.S.A., is one of the world's hottest places. Temperatures reach 56°C (133°F).

GRASSLANDS OF THE WORLD

- Grasslands cover about 34 million sq km (13 million sq miles) – about one-quarter of Earth's dry land. The world's grasslands started to develop during the Cretaceous period, about 70 million years ago.

- There are two main types of grasslands, temperate grasslands and savannahs, or tropical grasslands. About 7,500 different species of grasses grow in grasslands worldwide, but relatively few species of trees.

- Major temperate grasslands of the world include the North American prairies, the pampas of southern South America, and the steppes of Russia and Asia.

- Major tropical grasslands include the African savannah, the veld of South Africa, and the Brazilian campos.

Zebra graze on the Serengeti Plains in Africa.

FEATURES OF GRASSLANDS

- The Russian steppes stretch for about 8,000 km (4,960 miles) from Europe to central Asia.

- The wild grasslands of the steppes and American prairies have mostly been ploughed up and converted into farmland, for crops such as wheat, corn, oats, and barley.

- Grassland soil contains up to 20 per cent humus – the rich, fertile surface layer which provides nourishment for growing crops.

- Fires quite often break out in dry grasslands, whether started naturally by lightning, or accidentally by humans. They can be helpful because they kill shrubs that take nourishment from the soil, and clear the way for new growth.

- Grasslands are home to huge numbers of insects, birds, and reptiles, as well as burrowing rodents and other grazing mammals, such as deer. Large herds of zebra and wildebeest graze on the grasses of the Serengeti Plains in Tanzania, Africa.

Echidnas burrow in the grasslands of Australia.

FEATURES OF THE POLAR REGIONS

- The polar regions, the Arctic and Antarctic, lie in the far north and south of our planet. The curvature of the Earth means that the Sun's rays shine only weakly there, so it is always cold.

- The tilt of the Earth on its axis means that the far north and south are the "lands of the midnight sun", light for 24 hours a day in summer but dark for 24 hours a day in winter.

- Auroras are shows of shimmering lights seen in the night sky above the polar regions. In the Arctic they are known as the Northern Lights. They are caused by solar particles striking the atmosphere near the Poles.

Northern Lights, Alaska

POLAR EXPLORATION

Around 10,000 B.C. nomadic hunters from Arctic Russia and Scandinavia crossed to Alaska. From there they gradually spread east across Canada and Greenland.

983	Vikings from Scandinavia establish a colony on Greenland which lasts for several centuries.
1570s	European sailors including English explorers Martin Frobisher, Henry Hudson, and William Baffin explore the Arctic coast of Canada.
1720s	Russian explorers and Danish Vitus Bering map Siberia, and cross from Asia to Alaska.
1820	U.S. seal hunter Nathaniel Palmer and English sailor Edward Bransfield are among the first to sight the Antarctic continent.
1830s	English, French, and U.S. explorers chart the Antarctic coast.
1909	U.S. explorer Robert Peary and an Inuit team are first to reach the North Pole.
1911	Norwegian explorer Roald Amundsen is first to reach the South Pole.

THE ARCTIC

- The Arctic gets its name from the Greek word *Arktos*, meaning "bear", after the Great Bear constellation of stars which shines in the north.

- Most of the region inside the Arctic is covered by the icy Arctic Ocean. The northernmost parts of North America, Europe and Asia, and the huge island of Greenland also lie within the Arctic.

- The Arctic is rich in minerals, including coal, copper, iron, uranium, gold, and diamonds. Large oil and natural gas fields were discovered in Alaska, in northern U.S.A., in 1968.

- Fish and sea mammals thrive in the cold waters of the Arctic. Many types of birds and also caribou (reindeer) migrate to the far north to breed in spring.

Polar bear

THE ANTARCTIC

- The Antarctic is mostly occupied by land – the vast, frozen continent of Antarctica. It has never been inhabited by humans.

- Antarctica is the coldest, and also the windiest, place on Earth. Temperatures here drop to $-89°C$ ($-128°F$), the lowest ever recorded on Earth.

- Antarctica is Earth's highest continent, 2,400 m (8,000 ft) above sea level on average.

- The Antarctic's extreme cold means that no animals can survive inland all year round, but sea creatures thrive in the oceans around the coast – from tiny shrimp-like krill to fish, seals, walruses, whales, and seabirds such as penguins.

Penguin

- In winter, the landmass of Antarctica appears to get bigger as the seas around it freeze over. In summer as the sea ice melts, the continent seems to shrink.

Walrus

EXTREME WEATHER

DESTRUCTIVE HURRICANES

- Hurricanes (cyclones) are violent circular storms that mainly strike tropical coasts worldwide, including southeastern U.S.A., the Caribbean, Australia, Japan, and Bangladesh. Hurricanes are often given names, to help identify and track them.

- The world's most damaging hurricane, Hurricane Andrew, hit southeastern U.S.A. on 23–26 August, 1992. It caused an estimated $15 billion worth of damage (£8.8 million).

- The most powerful hurricane ever recorded, Hurricane Gilbert, struck the Caribbean in 1988. It had winds of up to 296 kph (184 mph), and killed 300 people.

- Cyclone Tracy hit Darwin, in northern Australia, on Christmas Day 1974. The entire town had be to rebuilt.

WORLD'S WORST TORNADOES

- Tornadoes are small but very violent, revolving storms that strike many parts of the world. They are most common in midwestern U.S.A., in a region called "Tornado Alley".

- An average of 850 tornadoes strike the U.S.A. each year, often in groups called swarms.

- In 1925, the American midwest was hit by powerful tornadoes that killed 792 people and injured 13,000.

- On 11 April, 1965, "Palm Sunday", a swarm of 51 tornados hit the midwest, killing 256 people. Some towns were struck several times during what is now called the "Palm Sunday Tornado Outbreak".

- On 26 April, 1989, the most destructive tornado ever recorded hit the town of Shaturia in Bangladesh, killing 1,300 people, and wrecking 50,000 homes.

A computer-generated image of Hurricane Fran, using data from weather satellites. Hurricane Fran struck North Carolina, U.S.A. in 1996.

DEADLY FLOODS

- Some of the world's worst-ever floods have been caused by hurricanes. In 1900, the town of Galveston, on an island off southern U.S.A., was hit by high seas after a hurricane. Waves washed over the island and 6,000 people drowned.

Seismic activity under
the water

Waves move across the
water at high speed

Tsunami wave crashes
onto the shore

- The river with the worst history of flooding is the Huang He (Yellow River) in eastern China. Over a million people died during a major flood there in 1887. The Yellow River flooded again in 1931 and 1938, killing thousands more people. Because of its terrible history, the river is known as "China's sorrow" .

- Tsunamis are tidal waves whipped up by a hurricane or, more often, by an underwater earthquake. On 13 November, 1970, tsunamis caused by a hurricane swept over islands in the Ganges Delta in Bangladesh. Over a million people died.

VIOLENT STORMS

- On 26 November, 1703, 8,000 people died when the "Great Storm" struck southern Britain.
- U.S. park ranger Roy Sullivan survived being struck by lightning seven times between 1942 and 1977.
- On 8 December, 1963, a Boeing 707 airliner was struck by lightning over Maryland, U.S.A., and crashed, killing 81 people. It was the world's worst disaster caused by lightning.
- Tororo in Uganda, East Africa, is the world's most thunder-prone region. In the ten years between 1967 and 1976, thunder rumbled there for an average of 251 days each year.
- On 26 November, 1970, 3.8 cm (1.5 in) of rain fell in a single minute in the most intense rain burst on the island of Guadeloupe in the Caribbean.

AVALANCHES

- In 218 B.C., the Carthaginian army led by Hannibal was crossing the Alps to invade the Roman Empire when it was hit by avalanches. A total of 18,000 soldiers and 2,000 horses died.

- In 1910, avalanches in Washington State, U.S.A., swept two trains off their tracks, killing 96 people. It was the worst avalanche disaster ever recorded in the U.S.A.

- On 13 December, 1916, 18,000 Austrian and Italian soldiers fighting in the Dolomite Mountains in Italy were killed by avalanches. Some of the avalanches were triggered by shots fired by the troops.

- In 1950–1951, 98 people died in a total of 1,100 avalanches in the European Alps, during the so-called "Winter of Terror".

- On 10 January, 1962, an avalanche on Mount Huascaran in the Andes, Peru, wrecked four villages and the town of Ranrahirca, leaving thousands of people homeless.

ICEBERGS AND SEA ICE

- On 15 April, 1912, the British luxury liner *Titanic* struck an iceberg in the northern Atlantic. The great ship sank, and around 1,517 people drowned.

- In 1915, the ship *Endurance*, carrying a British Antarctic expedition led by Ernest Shackleton, was trapped and crushed by sea ice off Antarctica. Shackleton and his men had to cross 1,500 km (930 miles) of stormy ocean in a tiny open boat to reach the safety of land.

- In 1989, the Russian ship *Maksim Gorkiy* was holed by sea ice when cruising off Iceland in thick fog. Luckily, helicopters managed to rescue everyone on board before the ship sank.

- In recent years, drifting icebergs have wrecked oil rigs in coastal waters off northern Canada and Alaska. Nowadays oil is drilled from floating platforms that can be towed away if a giant iceberg appears.

The largest mass of an iceberg is hidden below the surface.

MAJOR DROUGHTS

- A drought is a long period of unusually dry weather. Drought particularly threatens areas near deserts in hot regions worldwide, including India, Australia, and much of Africa.

- During a major drought in West Africa, in 1963, the Sahara Desert spread southward into a dry but fertile area called the Sahel. In 1985–1986, more than a million people in the Sahel died because of drought.

- In 1973–1974, 230,000 people died in droughts in Ethiopia and Somalia. In 1984, drought killed another 300,000 in East Africa.

- In 1982–1983, Australia was hit by a drought called "The Big Dry". In summer 1983, fire swept through a drought-stricken area near Melbourne in southeast Australia. It destroyed 330,000 hectares (815,100 acres).

- Since 1990, eastern Australia has suffered another major drought. Hundreds of farming families have been forced to leave land where crops can no longer be grown, or livestock reared.

BLIZZARDS AND HAILSTORMS

- During the bitterly cold winter of 1812–1813, blizzards overtook the army of French general Napoleon Bonaparte, who had invaded Russia. Fewer than ten per cent of Napoleon's 450,000 troops survived.

- The town of Paradise on the slopes of Mount Rainier in western U.S.A. is the snowiest place on record. In the 12 months between February 1971 and February 1972, it received 31 m (102 ft) of snow.

- In 1976–1977, blizzards struck Buffalo, New York, U.S.A. The snow drifts were up to 9 m (30 ft deep).

- The world's deadliest hailstorm struck the town of Moradabad in India on 20 April, 1888. The hailstones killed 246 people.

U.S. paramedic on emergency snow mobile

- On 14 April, 1986, a severe hailstorm hit Bangladesh. The hailstones weighed 1 kg (2 lb).

HUMAN INFLUENCE ON THE EARTH

POLLUTERS AND CONSUMERS

- The U.S.A. is the world's top energy consumer of fossil fuels and nuclear and hydro-energy. It is followed by China in second place, then Russia, Japan, and Germany.

- The United Arab Emirates emits more carbon dioxide gas (CO_2) per person than any other country. CO_2 contributes to global warming. The U.S.A. is the world's second largest CO_2 emitter per person, followed by Singapore and Kazakhstan.

- Brazil is felling its native forests more quickly than any other nation. Indonesia is the world's second-biggest tree-feller.

- The U.S.A. produces more waste per person than any other nation, followed by Australia, Canada, and Finland.

- Canada produces the most sulphur dioxide per person, followed by U.S.A., Germany, and UK. Sulphur dioxide causes acid rain.

The amount of household waste produced by the U.S.A. has doubled since 1972.

MAJOR HUMANMADE DISASTERS

- On 19 July, 1979, the world's worst oil spill occurred when two oil tankers collided off Trinidad in the Caribbean. Between them they spilled 280,000 tonnes (275,000 tons) of oil into the sea.

- On 26 April, 1986, a nuclear reactor exploded at Chernobyl in Ukraine, eastern Europe, polluting 28,000 sq km (10,900 sq miles). A cloud of radioactive material spread through Europe. Experts believe 6,000–8,000 people have died as a result.

- On 3 December 1984, a leak of poisonous gas from the Union Carbide factory in Bhopal, India, killed an estimated 3,500 people, one of the world's worst industrial disasters.

- On 24 March 1989, the tanker *Exxon Valdez* ran aground off the coast of Alaska, spilling 38,800 tonnes (38,024 tons) of oil. The spill damaged 2,093 km (1,300 miles) of coast.

MILESTONES IN CONSERVATION

- In 1972, representatives from 70 governments met at Stockholm, Sweden, to create the United Nations Environment Programme (UNEP). This organization puts pressure on governments to take better care of the natural world.

- In 1984, UNEP and other groups produced a World Conservation Strategy, and later a report called *Our Common Future*, aimed at conserving energy resources and curbing pollution worldwide.

- In 1988, UNEP set up a panel of international experts called the IPCC to assess the threat of global climate change.

- In 1992, at the Earth Summit in Rio de Janeiro, Brazil, many nations agreed to a Global Warming Treaty, limiting their emissions of the "greenhouse gases" that are causing rising temperatures worldwide.

- In 1997, the second Earth Summit in Kyoto, Japan, produced a new agreement to limit the release of greenhouse gases. However, some countries such as the U.S.A. have refused to sign the Kyoto agreement.

RESERVES AND NATIONAL PARKS

- Around the world, National Parks and wildlife reserves have been set up to protect wild areas from pollution and industrial development.
- The first National Park was Yellowstone in the Rocky Mountains, U.S.A. It was set up in 1872.
- In the U.S.A., 993,500 sq km (383,000 sq miles) of land is protected. That is over 10 per cent of the total.
- Brazil has the largest protected area of any country: 1,430,000 sq km (550,000 sq miles), 17 per cent of its total area.
- The whole continent of Antarctica is protected from mining and industrial development. The surrounding oceans are a sanctuary for whales.
- Australia's Barrier Reef is another major wildlife sanctuary, covering 300,000 sq km (116,000 sq miles) of ocean.

Yellowstone National Park

Glossary

ABYSSAL PLAIN
The deep, flat plain on the ocean floor.

ACID RAIN
Rain that is acidic due to pollution by sulphur dioxide and other gases.

ANTICYCLONE
Area of high atmospheric pressure.

ASTHENOSPHERE
Soft, semi-molten layer in the mantle on which the tectonic plates move. It is the layer under the lithosphere.

ATMOSPHERE
Envelope of air that surrounds the Earth. It can be divided into four layers: troposphere, stratosphere, mesophere, and thermosphere.

ATOLL
A circle of coral islands around a central lagoon.

AVALANCHE
A sudden, heavy fall of unstable snow, rock, or ice down a mountainside.

BAROMETER
An instrument that measures atmospheric pressure.

BEAUFORT SCALE
A twelve-step scale to gauge wind velocity based on the observable effects of the wind.

BASALT
The most common extrusive igneous rock. It is fine-grained and varies from dark grey to black in colour.

BEACH
Area between the cliffs or dunes and the lowest tides which is also known as the shore.

BIOSPHERE
Layer where life is found on Earth.

BLACK SMOKER
Chimney-like vent on the sea bed from which hot, black, mineral-rich water gushes.

BRECCIA
Sedimentary rock composed of coarse, angular rock fragments held together by a mineral cement.

CANYON
A deep valley with almost vertical sides, eroded by a river.

CFC
Chlorofluorocarbon containing carbon, chlorine, and fluorine. It is used in aerosol sprays, packaging, and refrigerators (see global warming).

CIRRUS CLOUD
Wispy white cloud made of ice crystals. It forms high in the atmosphere.

CLEAVAGE
A well-defined plane along which a mineral tends to break, related to weakness in the atomic structure of the mineral.

CLIMATE
The average weather conditions for a region over a long period of time.

CONTACT METAMORPHISM
Small-scale change of rock by heat as a result of close proximity to a body of magma or lava.

CONTINENTAL DRIFT
Theory suggesting that the Earth's continents have moved (drifted) relative to one another.

CORE
The innermost part of the Earth made of two layers: a solid inner core and a liquid outer core.

CRUST
The outermost layer of the Earth.

CUMULONIMBUS CLOUD
Tall storm cloud that often brings rain.

CUMULUS CLOUD
Fluffy cloud usually present in fine weather.

CYCLONE
An area of low atmospheric pressure. Also a tropical storm.

DEFORESTATION
Cutting down trees and clearing forests for crops, timber, and grazing land.

DESERTIFICATION
Creation of deserts by soil erosion through over-grazing, over-cultivation, or over-population.

ECOLOGY
The study of interactions between living organisms and their environment.

ECOSYSTEM
Communities of animals and plants dependent on each other and their environment to survive.

ENVIRONMENT
The living organisms and physical conditions in an area, including air, water, and soil.

EPICENTRE
Point on the Earth's surface directly above the focus of an earthquake.

EROSION
The removal of soil and weathered rock by flowing water, glaciers. or wind.

ESTUARY
Where fresh water mixes with sea water at the mouth of a river.

EXTRUSIVE IGNEOUS ROCK
Rock formed from lava erupted from volcanoes.

FIRN
Old, dense, granular compacted snow.

FISSURE ERUPTION
Volcanic eruption from a crack or linear vent in the ground.

FJORD
A former glacial valley with steep sides and a U-shaped profile, now occupied by sea water.

FOCUS
Point underground where an earthquake originates.

FOSSIL
Remains or traces of animals and plants preserved in rock.

FRACTURE
A break in a mineral or rock that is not related to its atomic structure.

FRONT
Area where two different air masses collide.

GLACIER
Mass of ice on land that flows downhill under its own weight.

GEYSER
A fountain of hot water or steam heated by volcanic activity.

GRANITE
A coarse-grained intrusive igneous rock.

GLOBAL WARMING (GREENHOUSE EFFECT)
An increase in the global temperature as a result of heat being trapped in the atmosphere by gases such as carbon dioxide.

GUYOT
Flat-topped submarine (undersea) mountain.

HABITAT
The environment in which an animal or plant lives.

HIGH
An area of high atmospheric pressure

HURRICANE
Violent tropical storm, also known as a cyclone, with high winds and torrential rain.

HOAR FROST
Water vapour from fog that crystallizes as ice on rough, cold surfaces.

IGNEOUS ROCK
Rock formed when magma or lava solidifies.

INTRUSIVE IGNEOUS ROCK
Igneous rock that has solidified beneath the Earth's surface.

ISOBAR
Line on a weather chart joining points with equal air pressure.

LAVA
Magma erupted from fissures and volcanoes.

LIGNITE
Soft, woody coal formed by the burial of peat.

LIMESTONE
Sedimentary rock, mostly calcium carbonate.

LITHOSPHERE
Outer layer of the Earth containing the crust and upper part of the mantle.

LONGSHORE DRIFT
The movement of sand and sediment along a beach by waves moving obliquely to the shore.

LOW
An area of low atmospheric pressure.

MAGMA
Molten rock material under the Earth's surface.

MANTLE
The thick layer between the core and the crust of the Earth.

MARBLE
A metamorphic rock, formed when limestone or another carbonate rock is changed by heat and/or pressure.

MERCALLI SCALE
Gives a value (1–12) for the magnitude of an earthquake based on its observed destructiveness.

METAMORPHIC ROCK
Rock formed by the effect of pressure and heat on existing rock.

METEOROLOGY
The scientific study of weather.

MID-OCEANIC RIDGE
The huge mountain range that runs through the middle of the oceans.

MINERAL
A naturally-occurring substance with a constant chemical composition and a crystalline structure.

ORBIT
The path taken by a planet as it travels around the Sun, or by a moon which travels around a planet.

ORE MINERAL
Mineral that contains enough metal to make its removal profitable.

OZONE LAYER
Layer in the upper atmosphere containing ozone, a gas that absorbs the Sun's harmful rays.

PALAEONTOLOGY
Scientific study of fossils.

PEAT
Dark soil formed by the partial decomposition of vegetation in wet areas of marsh or swamp.

PERMEABLE ROCK
Rock that allows water and other liquids, such as oil, to pass through it.

PLATE TECTONICS
A theory suggesting the crust is made of many rigid plates that move relative to each other.

POLLUTION
Substances, mostly deposited by humans, that contaminate the environment.

PRECIPITATION
Rain, sleet, hail, and snow, that fall to the ground from clouds.

PREVAILING WIND
The usual or common wind direction persisting in any one area.

RAINBOW
Coloured arc seen in the sky, formed when sunlight splits into the colours of the spectrum.

REGIONAL METAMORPHISM
Large-scale change of rock as a result of plate collision and mountain building.

RICHTER SCALE
A measure of earthquake intensity (0–10) based on the size of shock waves recorded on a seismograph.

RIFT (GRABEN)
Sinking of a strip of the Earth's crust between two faults.

ROCK
Solid mass made of one or more minerals.

SAVANNAH
Grassland area at the edge of the tropics which has seasonal rain.

SCREE
Mass of boulders and rock fragments that accumulates at the bottom of cliffs and mountain slopes.

SEISMIC WAVE
A shock wave from an earthquake, measured using a seismometer.

SEISMOLOGY
The study of earthquakes.

SMOG
A mixture of smoke and fog.

SOLAR SYSTEM
The Sun, and the planets, meteors, comets, moons, and asteroids orbiting the Sun.

SPREADING RIDGE
Submarine mountains where two plates are moving apart and new crust is being created.

STALACTITE
An icicle-shaped mineral deposit hanging from the roof of a cave.

STALAGMITE
Icicle-shaped mineral deposit that builds up from the cave floor.

STRATUS CLOUD
Low-lying, layered cloud.

STREAK
The colour of a mineral in its powdered form.

SUBDUCTION ZONE
Plane along which oceanic crust sinks beneath another plate.

TORNADO
Violent thunderstorm with a destructive funnel cloud and strong spiralling winds.

TRADE WINDS
Winds that blow from high pressure regions of sub-tropical belts towards areas of low pressure at the equator.

TSUNAMI
Destructive sea waves caused by earthquakes under the ocean.

VOLCANO
A vent in the Earth's crust through which magma is erupted as lava.

WEATHER
Atmospheric conditions at a particular time and place.

WEATHERING
Physical and chemical processes that break down rocks on the Earth's surface.

INDEX

Acknowledgments

Dorling Kindersley would like to thank:
DK Cartography for the maps, Hilary Bird for the index, and Chris Pellant for consulting on additional material.

Photographs by:
J. Stevenson, C. Keates, A. von Einsiedel, H. Taylor, A. Crawford, G. Kevin, D. King, S. Shott, K. Shone.

Illustrations by:
J. Temperton, J. Woodcock, N. Hall, R. Ward, E. Fleury, B. Donohoe, D. Wright, C. Salmon, B. Delf, P. Williams, S. Quigley, R. Shackell, R. Lindsay, P. Bull, P. Visscher, R. Blakeley, R. Lewis, L. Corbella, D. Woodward, C. Rose, N. Loates, G. Tomlin.

Picture credits: t=top b=bottom c=centre l=left r=right
AKG London: Erich Lessing / Galleria dell'Accademia 66bl. Bridgeman Art Library: British Museum 75bl; Christie's, London 46-47t. British Coal: 77tl. British Crown: 70tr. Bruce Coleman: G. Cubitt 75br; A.Davies 53bl, br; Dr M P Kahl 147cl; H. Lange 72-73; W Lawler 142t; Dr John MacKinnon 146tr; M Timothy O'Keefe 81b; Fritz Prenzel 55tl; Andy Purcell 137tr; Gunter Ziesler 146br. Ecoscene: A. Brown 50tl, 137br, 140-141; R. Glover 134bc; Pat Groves 117t; Sally Morgan 50bl, 60tr; Tweedie 66tl; P. Ward 144br. Mary Evans Picture Library: 30bl, 42c. Frank Lane Picture Agency: 34bl, H Hoslinger 139c; S. Jonasson 39cl; S. McCutcheon 40-41, 47bl; National Park Service 28-29. GeoScience Features Picture Library: 34tl, 37tr. Robert

Harding Picture Library: 48-49, 61tl, 91tl; D. Hughes 88tl; Krafft 36br; R. Rainford 84tl. Hulton Deutsch Collection: 75tl, 97bl, 122b, 132tr. Image Bank: 84bl, 86br; L. Brown 124-125; G. Champlong 120t; T Madison 59tl; B. Roussel 135c. Mountain Camera: J. Cleare 30tl. Museo Archeologico Nazionale di Napoli back cover cr. NASA: 8-9, 138tr, 150-180, 150tl, 162-163, 176-177. National History Museum: 63bc, 64cl, 65bl. National Maritime Museum 169tr, cr. Oxford Scientific Films: Ben Osborne 144bl. Planet Earth: J. Downer 122t; J. Fawcett 38tl; R. Hessler 39tr; C. Huxley 2tr, 100-101; J. Lithgoe 96tr; B. Merdsoy 92-93; W. M. Smithey 91bl; N. Tapp 88bl. Rex Features: A. Fernandez 35t; SIPA Press 44tl. Royal Navy Submarine Museum 169br. Science Museum, London: 147b. Science Photo Library: D. Allan 90t; Tony Craddock 82-83; Dan Farber 138br; S. Fraser 137bl; J. Heseltine 52tl; D. Pellegrini 98tr; Dr Morley Read 144tl; NASA 110; F. Sauze 104tr; US Geological Survey 20-21. Solarfilma: 36tr. Frank Spooner Pictures: Barr/Liaison 34br; Garties/LN 37tl; Vitti/Gamma Liaison. Tony Stone Images: 58t, 60br, 78tr, 80tr; T. Braise 123b. Volunteer Medical Service Corps, Lansdale 179br. Tony Waltham: 30cl, 32tl, 114-115. L.White, 116t. Zefa: 46br, 86cl, 136t, 145tc.

Every effort has been made to trace the copyright holders and we apologize in advance for any unintentional omissions. We would be pleased to insert the appropriate acknowledgment in any subsequent edition of this publication.